Other Seasons

Other Seasons

Harold J. Recinos

RESOURCE *Publications* · Eugene, Oregon

OTHER SEASONS

Copyright © 2017 Harold J. Recinos. All rights reserved. Except for brief quotations in critical publications or reviews, no part of this book may be reproduced in any manner without prior written permission from the publisher. Write: Permissions, Wipf and Stock Publishers, 199 W. 8th Ave., Suite 3, Eugene, OR 97401.

Resource Publications
An Imprint of Wipf and Stock Publishers
199 W. 8th Ave., Suite 3
Eugene, OR 97401

www.wipfandstock.com

PAPERBACK ISBN: 978-1-5326-1104-9
HARDCOVER ISBN: 978-1-5326-1106-3
EBOOK ISBN: 978-1-5326-1105-6

Grateful thanks is made to David E. Schmersal, Reference and Digital Services Librarian of the Bridwell Library, Perkins School of Theology, Southern Methodist University, for assisting with the book cover.

Manufactured in the U.S.A.

Contents

[The Lost Season]	1
[For You]	2
[China Town]	3
[Lost Key]	4
[Psalm 137]	5
[The Mural]	6
[Clouds]	7
[The Amusement Park]	8
[The Blue Note]	9
[Yard Sale]	10
[Breakfast]	11
[Evening Prayer]	12
[The Return]	13
[9/11]	14
[The Letter]	15
[The Bum]	16
[The Candle Store]	17
[The Prayer]	18
[Wandering]	19
[The Barrio]	20
[Hispanic Heritage Month]	21
[The Way to School]	22
[The Woman in the Factory]	23
[Sacred]	24
[The Star]	25
[The Longing]	26
[Missing]	27
[Away]	28
[Old Women of Summer]	29
[The String]	30
[Campesino]	31
[The Block]	32
[English Tongues]	33
[Prayer Night]	34
[A Dove at the Station]	35
[The University]	36
[Playing]	37
[The Long Arm of Hate]	38
[Colors]	39
[The Moon]	40
[The School Visit]	41
[My Love]	42
[The Stroll]	43
[The Television]	44
[The Watch Fixer]	45
[Rice Rain]	46
[There you Stand]	47
[Saturday Night Confession]	48
[Waiting]	49
[The Pew]	50
[The Politician]	51
[The Convention]	52
[Forgotten Civil War]	53
[Soul]	54
[The Opera]	55
[First Day of School]	56
[I Take Your Hand]	57
[The Valley]	58
[Lost and Found]	59
[Mission]	60
[The Post Office]	61
[When the Angels Come]	62
[Holy Night]	63
[The Living Room]	64
[The Disappeared]	65
[Once A Wish]	66
[Homeless]	67
[New Shoes]	68
[Lead Me]	69
[The Chevy]	70
[Awake]	71
[A Mother Gone]	72
[Morning]	73
[The Refugee Woman]	74

Contents *(continued)*

[Store Front Church]	75	[The Flower Pot]	103
[They Came]	76	[Dead End Street]	104
[The Night Club Shooting]	77	[The Factory Floor]	105
[The Window View]	78	[Works of Love]	106
[June Morning]	79	[Street Light]	107
[In Memory]	80	[Fourth of July]	108
[The Caged Bird]	81	[Stand]	109
[The Blessing Box]	82	[The Morning News]	110
[The Poet's Street]	83	[Politics]	111
[Absent Father]	84	[The Bus]	112
[The Refugee Family]	85	[A Short Walk]	113
[The First Poem]	86	[The Orange]	114
[The Waiting Room]	87	[Sunday]	115
[So far Away]	88	[The Subway Station]	116
[Still Night]	89	[War]	117
[Independence Day]	90	[Darling]	118
[Holding Hands]	91	[Caged Bird]	119
[East River End]	92	[Lost]	120
[The Wall]	93	[The Fire]	121
[Another Country]	94	[Recalling]	122
[Brown River]	95	[The Talk]	123
[Sugarcane]	96	[The Bronx]	124
[Walk Around the Lake]	97	[The Book]	125
[March with Us]	98	[The Game]	126
[Exit Wound]	99	[Walking Home]	127
[They Tremble to Sleep]	100	[Talk]	128
[Summer Break]	101	[The Pigeon-Man]	129
[The Fire Escapes]	102	[The Choir]	130

[The Lost Season]

I will read you the lost words
of the ancient texts that turned

the earth, made the hoarse birds
sing, and gave us tongues to speak

in ways to make even the sly devil
sick. I will read to you of the warming

sun, the wide-mouthed sky, the silver
speckled night, the beauty of the moon

the very first eyes on earth to see. I will
read to you the stories of the singing rain,

the flowing rivers it loves, the vast seas
that never say enough. I will read about

the ageless blowing wind, the trees standing
serene, the flowers like sweet lovers generous

with time, and you will know before we
close the book life once had no complaints,

not a drop of blood was shed, there was no
war, or corpses bundled on the corner of

village streets. I will read to you with my
trembling lips the whole and brilliant spell

of original peace.

[For You]

for you who labor hard all day
then go home to bend your knees
in prayer for the dispossessed with
beautiful dark skin. for you who
struggle in the solemn houses of
God, are discriminated on the job,
in the schools, the local shops, the
doctor's office, the hospitals, the cops,
on the buses, and trains, yet are never
chained by it. for you who have the
strength to sweep the halls, empty rubbish
bins, trim the lawns, plant flowers, harvest
crops, care for children, wash clothes, iron
shirts, and cook to make life easier for others
with means who never think to make you
a little more rich. for you who grow up to
become Supreme Court judges, astronauts,
scientists, Senators, composers, musicians,
novelists, artists, poets, ballerinas, actors,
teachers, therapists, plumbers, electricians,
masons, carpenters, preachers, athletes, priests
and nuns, high achievers in all the fields kept
closed to us, even president. for you who walk
the shady streets spreading joy, who rest homeless
on the park benches still drinking to confess, shoot
dope on rooftops to find home, who manage laughter
no matter how tangled life becomes with bunched
up crap. for you I cry to all the Gods in heaven
with a raised triumphant fist.

[China Town]

I walked down Canal Street
where grocers sell fish from iced

tables in front of their stores that
have strange Chinese names. a sign

nearly unseen behind a plump Buddha
in one of them read *se habla español*.

three Puerto Rican ladies were inside
the place smiling beside a tank with live

catch saying names unheard by the
merchant's tongue that came to New York

from the Far East. I stopped on the loud
sidewalk in front of the shop to smile at

them from the ordinary shadows of
the market street. I walked further along

the block aware it was nearly night and
soon the stars would turn on above the

city's rooftops daring us to sleep and
stroking park vagrant's hair with a gentle

breeze. I walked by a man playing blue
melodies on a worn violin to the banks

where the Hudson River spreads to enjoy her
flashy current rushing swiftly, there I imagined

lives past, present and still to come to share in
this world. I sat to catch my breath looking across

the brown waters and allowed the coming
night to drop peace on me like Bronx Angels'

sing.

[Lost Key]

I was walking on a quiet day thinking
of a lost key listening to Mourning Doves

announce the rising light with song. I could
smell a faint touch of perfume on the lady

with long black hair in a white dress walking
in front of me waking me up. I decided to

stroll long enough to remember the whereabouts
of the key to the apartment with heckling grey

radiators in the building none of the neighbors
liked. I walked by St. John's Chrysostom Church

wondering what not keeping the Sabbath had to
do with this lost key and decided to wander in to

light a few candles. I sat in the third pew for a few
moments listening to a priest who happened to sing,

hoping my crowded head would remember this of all
things. I wanted to grow old with that key, have it

unlock my Eden whenever needed for a taste of peace,
and let it store sweet memories in rooms I alone would

enter. no matter how hard I thought the key did
not come back to me, I cried for ancient tongues

to speak the secret of lost objects, and kept walking
around like a child in search of Jerusalem in the Bronx

for the tiny little opener with a red dot on it that
would open my mother's apartment door—home

to me. I still foolishly yearn to find it in a sidewalk
crack, beneath an old cushion at church, on an altar

in a grocery store with plastic Saints, or in the pocket
of the last domino player on the block who will say

I found it!

[Psalm 137]

by the rivers along the border, we
sat and wept with memories of the

villages that taught us to believe
in happiness. there under the cashew

trees, we frolicked in the evening glow
with music played on strings the soldiers

one day would toss in an impetuous stream
they watched turn red with our blood. how

can we sing on the other side of this river
in the North? where is our highest joy,

the holy ground, the Lord that will repay
them for our weaknesses and deaths? when

will our stammering tongues sing again to
send away those who stomp us to the ground

in this foreign place? what peace will come to
us, now? what justice will overtake the owners

of this world and their fallen souls? who will
remember us like cherished flowers to be held?

cursing the violence of war, on this river bank,
vengeance is not our dream, life is the truest

thing we bid to put an end to the threats hanging
above our heads and dropping us without tears

into fresh foreign earth.

[The Mural]

ablaze, the candles burned
beside the wall of Big Pun
with flowers around them,
the kids stood in front of the
mural with bowed heads glad
to praise the one who sang against
the jeering eyes uptown, the disapproving
priests, and an angry God who they
say forgets to save. the mother big
with another child, holding a little girl's
hand, stared at the wall like someone
seeing into a mirror waiting for truth to
ripen in her eyes. when her lips began
moving the gathered listened to her
say Mr. Rios we have passion left to
love the block, you remain sweet for
for us and the children like to stop in
front of this wall to cobble hope and
rap. in the silence of the afternoon,
before the crowd dispersed, a prayer
was said to remember the secrets of our
brown skin ancient like dark mother
earth.

[Clouds]

its late into the night of this
August summer and I sit quietly
with closed eyes feeling all the
years behind me without a thought
in mind. I put down a book that
made good company filled with
an inexplicable happiness the stories
of Julio Cortázar succeed to deliver.
in the dark, enjoying the light of a
small lamp, I imagine voices shouting
from pages to describe the clouds hiding
a sky full of stars, leaves rustling in near
autumn trees, lovers parting again with
unbearable regret, and a child about to
speak. I lean forward like someone in a
mystery waiting for words to lunge from
the dark, which in great stories, find many
ways to say you are beloved on earth.

[The Amusement Park]

the rain stopped, and the Sunday dress
kids in the building waiting it out, begin

to walk quickly in the damp air toward
church like people with unfinished

business. time in Tito's pocket ticked
loud enough for him to clinch his hand

around a strapless watch before it got
all used up. they waited patiently for God

to speak each Sunday but only noticed the
priest a little more bald, widows dressed

in black, babies loudly crying, young girls
with scarves covering their long hair, and

most of the block praying for another Paradise.
their hearts that morning were already in the

amusement park sitting on the side of a
New Jersey cliff, inviting them on Easter to

fly beneath the clouds in wild rides to make
them hold the air. with their eyes closed in the

middle of Mass where a little bell sounds ringing
faults, they whispered to each other imagine what

it would be like to have to spend the day here and
never Palisades Amusement Park. when the tolling

bell stopped, the six friends popped their eyes open
and dashed to happiness waiting on the other side of

the church front door. despite the raggedy sermon
not one of them felt mortified, the slightest bit lost

or need for Christ's salvation—maybe next year the
priest will convince them to forget the sinful times

at Palisades Amusement Park and see things,
otherwise.

[The Blue Note]

I liked coming out of the Blue Note
that autumn night with the long slow

walk past people sitting on the slanted
benches of Washington Square Park,

the occasional leaf tumbling down on
the heads of kids riding skateboards,

students marking pages in their books,
the middle-aged chess players focused

on a game, and on the south end of the park
toddlers shrieking with attempted swings on

a jungle gym. I looked up at the night sky
convinced I could reach out to polish the

stars to help them cast more gracious light
on every toiler here. slowly, I made my

way down half-deserted streets trying not
to step on the sidewalk cracks, nearing

home, I prayed for Eden's distant friends
led astray and looked on all the quiet corners

for stirs of sweet life.

[Yard Sale]

early one morning in front of Leroy's
ground floor apartment a sidewalk sale

was underway with a baby crib, records, two
chairs, a desk lamp, an old bicycle, worn clothes,

a broken-handle toaster and a checker set. the
Irish lady who put the sale together hoped to

get a little business from the new Puerto Rican
residents pouring out of a storefront church, though

they never heard a Doris Day record, asked what is
checkers, and reserved an entirely different taste in

clothes. Leroy told me his mother hatched the idea
to earn a little money to help pay the rent before the

family lost its roof and had to sleep beneath a street
of stars. I never imagined pale faced poor till then, so

I gathered the Nuyorican shoe shine boys on the block,
told them they best pray up better days for redheaded

Leroy with Saint Patty's name, then convinced them
to drop a quarter in a cup to buy the life line checker

set. when somebody bought the desk lamp the look
in the Irish mother's eyes was like an Angel came by

saying do not be afraid you will be paid with scanty
Spanish speaking cash, instead of city dust. on that

day, I swear the multicolored poor on the block
could not have loved each other more with the very

simple kindness the rest of the world did not care
to give.

[Breakfast]

she starts the day listening to the
news in the tiny kitchen of a two

room apartment, the motions of
her hand stirring Oatmeal her kids

will eat for breakfast before walking a
long way to school in the company

of the morning wind. without thinking
about her misery she manages to say a

little pray to the Mother of Peace to
request mercy for the ladies on the

block who look into the faces of their
children every day hoping they will know

years of perfect life. when you look deeply
into her eyes you will find in them something

no one on the block can completely give, a thing
in her that never fades, an ancient presence like

the stones on the empty lot about to speak, the
clouds crowning school children's heads, or Angel's

come to earth for play—the simple miracle of love.

[Evening Prayer]

in the wilderness of the soul, God is present.
in human imperfection, God is present.
in the mystery of consciousness, God is present.
in the forgiveness of things, God is present.
in the kind gesture of welcoming love, God is present.
in the simplicity of childish things, God is present.
in the incurable laughter of being, God is present.
in misery turned hope, God is present.
If not here, then nowhere.

[The Return]

I don't understand a thing about yesterday
though it must be around somewhere the

eye simply cannot see. sometimes I wonder
if it will catch up to me with a strong rain, reach

out from a dim place in the middle of the night insisting
on talking about domestic affairs, or have me simply sit in

a chair to listen to bygone events like they were happening
fresh over again. I don't understand a thing about the way

yesterday takes on light to appear with missing friends risen
again who slowly walk up a road broadening in my mind where

they meet me like it's the first time. I don't understand why
nearly everything swallowed by yesterday is nearly forgotten,

like the six transistor radio that fit in a pocket, the cheap
wine kids drank to ritually spew, the wide-eyed mornings

with rice soup eaten before long walks to the English only
school, the box full of books about other worlds that vanished

into air, and the small good things that helped our captive
time leak dreams. I quit counting yesterday, turned away from

its disappearing act, and vowed to walk like Tito's blind uncle
tapping my way around the forward turning hands of the clock

toward what the future brings. who knows I may well understand
yesterday and all the faulty things it stores coming finally
unmasked

for me.

[9/11]

how many seconds, minutes, hours, days, weeks,
months, years ago did the world on a Tuesday

morning bleed? how many remember the night before
everything changed by showing us what loathed

human flesh can become? Will the multiplying death
piled on many mountains now of splintered bones ever

bring us peace? we are up early with our grief talking
of these things in a world distorted by crooked views

of God and the innocent who were killed. today, we
will go to the places where hell appeared with black

flowers to hear prayers calling for blessings and the
fullness of peace, then with choking faith in heaven

will silently shake our heads. the day it happened,
still covered in ash, makes the light grow thin for

us—the ears torn off still listen.

[The Letter]

the future, is resting
on the steps of the old

building with chipped
bricks, where the old man

likes to sit to stare at windows
on the other side of the street.

in his pocket buried deep is an
unopened letter from a love still

wept that long ago descended into
a still dark. a child takes a place

beside him and with an upward glance
smiles for his older eyes, making any

semblance of sadness on the stoop take
flight. together they sat jumping over

shadows, searching for spots on the sidewalk
that glowed, and laughing about the Summer

drifting away. for hours they kept company
greeting the changing day, naming creatures

in the clouds slowly floating by, feeling love
moved to offer the changing tides a gentle peace

costing nothing to believe.

[The Bum]

he walked the city streets looking
at the wandering priests, mothers,

dealers, junkies, and aging drunks
who live in different worlds. they

looked like strangers to him carved
from simple clay, names of flesh

and bone, tossed across the altars
of the earth, and planted with too

many longings. sometimes, he
imagined whispering to their wintered

hearts a world of things about sleeping
in a cardboard box, the wine bottle in

his exhausted hands, the family he no
longer knows, and the burning-bush of

nightly dreams that does not speak.
when his huge beggar eyes teared with

sparrows infinitely near, you could
see him sunk in silence finally whisper God

is hunger, not love.

[The Candle Store]

I walked past the house of candles
that tells us to think dutifully of light,

to search the spreading night with blue
flames, to find warmth for the feverish

words that tug within. I saw a magician
looking around in front of the store with

a small group closing the day with laughter
given by tricks. on the faces of the candle

buyers you could see a curtain gently part
to disclose bells ringing above their heads

sounds of kindness. I stare up the street to
the place that makes us bend our heads real

low, where the silence received another son,
and the Great Will that pines for the loud world

has not yet come. tonight, I care about our
weeping, not the sun, the moon, the stars, the

deep sea, the mountains forested in green. I
light candles for the most loved, the lost, the

mothers weary of sleep, the beautiful brown
faces not yet born that will walk this way some

day. I will stand still now with the candle in
my hand praying for the tiny flame to lift our

spirits high above the thinning air for a taste
of peace.

[The Prayer]

on the way to the corner church
whenever he walked pass the store

window with the broken flower pots,
in him something shouted a concern for

prayer, a need to hurry up to kneel at the
altar rail to speak to the teacher who wrote

in sand disclosing eternal truth. beyond the
discords of a wounded world and deep in

the roaming of his heart, the radiant images
of infants in their mother's arms interpreting

love in shadowy pews comes to him. inside
the space where the Mother of Heaven has

made her residence, he gets as close to the Holy
One at the foot of a simple wood cross as flesh

permits. on the way back to his apartment where
the regrets of many seasons are kept, he admits

there will never be an end to his thanks for the
magnificent cause of being delivered on the ruinous

Golgotha hill—in daily thirst for light he once
again emerges deeply moved.

[Wandering]

I have walked the streets of many
cities, flown to many places, slept

in foreign parks, pretended to have
a home in cracked spaces across a

thousand shores, found people beside
me say nothing of stumbling with

sorrow, melancholy junkies with a
taste for cheap wine drunk after a

numbing fix. I have seen people in
the barrio unconcerned with where

they live lose sight of their dearest
dreams and get lowered into earth.

I have wandered neighborhood cemeteries
shaking my head at graves with notes

taped to headstones and colorful flowers
with rotting petals the things left behind

to scream regret. I have known the
taste of absence, the obscenities of faith,

the church dropped into darkness, and my
soul thickly sick. I wait for the stainless

days when the low voice of the beggar
in rags at the end of a dark street calls

your life is moored to another shore so
stand up—I walk now for the sake of

him.

[The Barrio]

in the barrio the walls sing, whistles
blow for kids playing on the street,
rice slowly cooks on stoves in kitchens
smelling of yesterday's saintly feast.
shopping bag *abuelas* dream of big
houses with pale maids that cannot
speak a word of Spanish, children with
private tutors sitting on the plastic slip
covered sofas educating dreams, a world
with brown lives rolling in justice and free.
in the barrio, my brown hands searched the
dark for light, found one brighter than the
sun, and will not let it go.

[Hispanic Heritage Month]

we have gathered words these
many years to write letters to

spread across the sky until the
end of time. the voices rise in

the harvest fields, they carol
songs from histories ground to

the deaf of ear, speak heaven's
dreams to those who labor in the

kitchen, patching tires, fixing cars,
building things, packing meat, serving

food, harvesting crops, laying bricks,
mending pipes, nailing wood, stretching

wire, playing sports, raising kids, teaching
school, holding court, leading Mass, healing

the sick, and marching to old Uncle Sam's
beating drum. we have gathered this month

with aged blood-shot eyes to remind
America of her beautiful brown skin and

a history magnificently chatted for hundreds
of years in Spanish. we have gathered on

the white porches calling for liberty to come
out, loathing to be carried away in chains, and

invisibility to plunge without halting a single
step into the deepest grave. we have gathered

to tell you with perfect broken-hearted dreams
America through all our deeds is the place we

rumble loud for home, justice, belonging and
peace.

[The Way to School]

the street I walked to school was
dense with old buildings without a single

tree planted in front, liquor stores were
on every other block, and winos who sang

ABC'S out loud for school kids to hear. on the
way, I wondered why tourists never strolled down

this street taking pictures of unemployed vets who
questioned after hammering tiny countries down

coming back to sit on sidewalks drinking cheap
wine and pledging allegiance with their slurring

tongues. at the school, teachers pushed smiles to
lips but never heard a story from a neighborhood

resident louder than a foolish whim. I never could
imagine why our different voices were so routinely

drowned—perhaps, you will tell me?

[The Woman in the Factory]

this woman has worked the morning
cutting zippers on a press without a

break, beads of sweat dripping from
her brow, and the hands that buttoned

her daughter's Catholic school white
blouse, with dirt now beneath the nails.

quietly, she sees the dust on the factory
floor kicked up by the feet of the supervisor

with a cracked voice who for the last twenty
years has waited for a different job. she has

moved around the dim rooms of this work
place with a long list of nameless wage workers

who drank themselves to death. in her eyes you
can see the last shift sweetly rising and a closer

look discloses her long brown hands gently
lifted with piety to heaven for joy to come.

the other dust like her working the assembly line
with dreams of what lies ahead will soon see

not many more days will keep them from the
place this woman's yearning soul visits for light.

quietly, after work she returns to the little girl sent
to school, the shared love, words and a delicious

single mom life.

[Sacred]

I noticed one afternoon sitting
on the stoop the quiet figure of
an old woman looking left and
right like she was about to reveal
something. centuries ago her
ancestors inhaled the mysteries
reflected through her wrinkled
eyes, they built the sacred cities
in the forests and the clouds, and
charted the movement of the stars.
and now this treasure sits on the
stoop next to me drying children's
tears.

[The Star]

when the oldest star shines in heaven
to announce the coming visit, I will

look out the window for the hunched
old women, the junkies they fear, the

mothers who are hustling, the children
with tough questions and the excluded

on the streets. together, we will sing the
ancient ways to have you come nearer,

before our time is done. I will build a
cart for sorrows to collect the worried

news, every word that stumbles, the
cries for the forgiveness of the block's

dead. I will walk the night with the
staring sky to knock on the weeping

doors, invite the aging forgers, trampled
prostitutes, unrepentant gangsters, predators,

murderers, thieves, even tired old priests,
to line up for bread in your passionate world

that comes. when the oldest star goes forth
in the sky, I will climb the tallest building

to cry like Hannah from the heart for you to
listen.

[The Longing]

the streets have grown a little older,
the wails of infants walked in strollers

hardly ever heard, the old Jewish
fiddler who played the alleys with

music from another world has long
been dead, the priest who everyone

said had kept a trench on his tongue
for just in case days was lifted to

paradise, and the piragüeros on the
boulevard come from Mexico, now.

when you forget what it was like on
the block come visit to stand in front of

Henry's building that still has a Big H
painted on the second floor wall, lean against

the telephone building to remember smoke
billowing from the rooftops, music on hot

nights played on fire escapes, and what
scratching the bottom of the rice pot said of

hunger on the block. I come back each year
like a confessed sinner to pass time on the

wounded corners, to whisper to the clouds
the names of people with nothing left, gone

and crippled friends, and mothers who used
only words to reveal the limitless dreams they

had sewn in us. I will wait for you here in
the places you know are sweetly followed

by light.

[Missing]

I went out to look for you
crossing a dozen streets,

roving the alleys, visiting
the rooftops on Longfellow

Avenue, asking thrown away
needles, burnt bottle caps, and

scattered empty dope bags to
give you away. into the city

night, I knocked on the secret
doors of the abandoned tenements,

where people live who left homes
long ago cursing the wind, to ask of

your whereabouts. the windows on
the old buildings trembled, and no

one could say. I made my way to
the avenue, stopped in front of the

grocery store with a candle's light
flickering in front of a Saint. the

cripple and the hurt are always brought
to him for healing in the dark church,

but I heard a voice saying invite San
Martin to stroll the streets to disrupt

the silence keeping you hid. I realized
when I finally found you at the hospital

dead that heaven has deaf ears for
junkies like you—Mother of God,

I cried!

[Away]

he went to another country in a van
full of Salvadorans ready to move into

the apartment Leo kept alone for years
in Washington, D.C. the girls he left at

home would find their way North holding
hands all the way to the capital city at a later

date—he dreamed. neighbors in his building
say they hear him sing in the sweetest tenor

voice protest songs each evening to reminiscence
about the sweet lips, soft hands, tender hearts and

whisperings of the dead. when in the parking
lot of the convenience store full of prayers about

being picked for day labor, he carries the shanty
town of the dark world that raised him, and puts

together memories of that place the way he left,
when the moon hugging the mountains cast a

silver light on his departure. thousands
of miles away he smiles at the same blowing

wind, the stars that know his name, and the
bright sun that generously looks down on this

spinning mass of rock. no one in the building
has asked him about the parting, the nights alone

with his avalanche of tears, nor why he stands
nightly by the window staring at the dusty park

below? most likely, he would find countless ways
to say everything is well. yet, he knows that back

in Leo's place in the dark of his room, chains will
rattle to remind him of how far this strange land is

from everyone and everything beloved.

[Old Women of Summer]

on this lean summer day it is clear to
me like the flight of the red-winged

black bird that draws the darkness away
from streets, the lonely old church is still

the place the old women visit to fetch
hope for the week and drink a fill of

living water. the sweat of their brows has
touched the earth more times than anyone has

ever thought to count, they have crossed more
borders than had dreams, and like a Garcia Marquez

novel where life in sullied village huts is told, they
lean into life to speak to the world about us. when these

old women fall into exile moving around the neighborhood
without tears, short of prayers, with hearts to bitter to lay

blame, something in them begins to tick louder than the
biggest city clocks. time and again, in them we see there

is no end, and the look in their wrinkled eyes speak to
us like language of the living colors of the world that not

a single yellow day of summer can withstand. on this lean
hot day, I must confess to loving the stupendous simplicity

of these old women who live with the most exquisitely quilted
love that sticks to their brown skin and makes us bend easily to

them.

[The String]

the pigeons perched on telephone lines
recited their lines with the wind blowing
strongly to ruffle their feathers and the sun
disappearing for the third time behind a swift
passing cloud. never overtaken by sadness they
watch the slow moving day, water tossed out of
a window, a woman dressed in white selling
sweets from a cart, laughing girls skipping rope
in front of the building where the old man with
a patch over his left eye sits at night to talk about
his days in El Salvador playing first violin. I rest
for a moment on the street that will always possess
my life, like a weak salsa dancer trying to catch
a breath, thinking about the last time I saw you
on the block heading to the triple feature movie
house on Southern Boulevard to watch a bunch of
Dean Martin flicks. I hear you making witty
chatter with the girl who lives on West Farms Road
that everyone says has the mildest eyes in the city and
a smile that speaks better than a Sunday Mass about
giving. the years have galloped with fewer dreams
fed, the block will never change back the clocks,
and when I paused on the corner something of the
glory of last summer days said your face has not yet
fallen to bone—soon, we can catch up to tie strings.

[Campesino]

I listened beneath the shade of the tall
tree in the village square to the tale of an

elderly peasant about God humbly appearing
to become acquainted with people in the

the clearing who lived bent with humiliation
and trembling with fear. I looked into his eyes

searching them for answers about how to make
life perfect. the tiny church's bells began ringing

and tears filled his eyes to carry the agony of
his beaten up humanity, then he offered a few more

words saying kindness is the secret we must share
in order to justly, fearlessly, humbly, and peaceably

live. by the time I finished talking with the old
man, I could feel darkness fall and I swear the

humble God who allowed himself to die sat with
us in the shade of that tree.

[The Block]

I came back to the block and know it
now for the first time without a needle

in my veins, children dealing drugs, Lefty
drowning in his blood, the priest with the

altar boy in a room far from God, the old
restaurant where the shoe shine boys met

to eat flan. I came back to the block to see
lowly people helping each other find bread,

living in buildings slowly tumbling down, and
putting flowers on a mural painted on a wall

of an avenue to give courage. I came back
to the block hoping once again to find on its

busiest corner a sign from above disclosing
the last wretched days were nearer to us than

the sweet homemade coconut ice cream sold
from carts by the old women on the block. I

will return again and again to breathe on these
streets.

[English Tongues]

I am trying to probe all I know about
the English tongues that convey stories

about border crossers they know at
a distance and do not understand. for

some reason they rarely say a thing of
the darkness torn away by those who

walk the villages in fright and cross
the river thinking of all they leave.

they have an almost religious way of
hurling monstrous words of negation

for the poor who slide over the wall, float
on water to our shores, or ride across the

border with their beautiful brown flesh. I
am trying to understand why they never speak

of the long arms of God stretched for the
despised, why the silence about village

women disappeared in the dark, or children
greeted with bullets to the head. I am trying

to understand why these English speaking
tongues want to rub out the only words worthy

for our great city streets . . . . .Come in!

[Prayer Night]

one night after the pounding rain,
by the east river docks, when the old
church bells were eagerly hollering
for a penitent crowd, we gathered
beneath a glinting moon for a time
of prayer. a white haired man, painted
like a clown, wearing a costume with large
red buttons who had just finished working the
Elder Avenue subway stop, joined the group
with a far off look in his eyes. the wind blowing
wild made the red flowers in his left hand dance
until he gave one to each of the elderly ladies out
in the spreading dark for praise. around half-past
the hour, the people working the night shift
at the toy factory ever since they crossed the
border, walked over to rejoice in the words
the simple gathering of evangelists lifted up to
heaven to keep from perilously living deaf, blind
and mute. we have prayed for years on that very
spot with elated hearts recovering the imperfect
good news peddled by a homeless God—we will
do it again next week.

[A Dove at the Station]

a white dove just flew onto the
subway platform from the only
tree growing beside the entrance
to the station. the bird did not
leap out of the pages of the bible
to find rest here, though I wondered if
this creature was part of the definite
sign of God Borges saw with closed eyes
in a flock? Could it be the little dove
came to this station to tell us the Bronx is
easily forgotten by the winged? I watched a little
longer, looked up and down the subway platform,
and decided this bird was just a simple little
dove with no extraordinary gifts to drop on our
heads. before the next train arrived, I watched
her skip around then fly away from us, forever.
the little bird turned into a tiny speck in the
sky and that made me shake my head thinking
I love you more right now than heaven though
for that some will pray me damned.

[The University]

he was a student at the University where
armed men in uniforms gunned down

Jesuits, a mother and young girl for the
way they believed, thought and worked.

in classrooms, he learned a gospel the
governors were killing with every bullet

they could find, the curses they hurled,
and all the dirty work that money fueled

to keep soldiers acting on their lies. he
learned from the priests the sorrows of the

poor, the hollow hearts of the coffee growing
class, and the service of the military to them.

he was a student at the University in a country
named after a Galilean Jew who not even in a

wild dream would believe that in a pious country
those who loved the poor would be killed by

so many confessing to follow him. he was a student
with priests who served the despised and that is why

he walks with the poor despite the wealthy still
dreaming up newer rousing lies that now aim at

him.

[Playing]

I like it when the kids on
the block rush into the light

of the last working street lamp
in the neighborhood beating their

arms like wings, while people pass
along in bicycles, cars and buses

thinking life is never dull. when they
kick up the city dust in games filling the

air with intoxicating laughs there isn't
a single soul around with roots not deeply

stirred. they talk to me of things they
know are true and I have come to see

like earthly bonds of friendship that cling
despite harsh storms beneath the winking

stars. I see them skipping through the night,
singing in the city's kindest time, in shadows

tenderly near and mixed up with the most
honest part of me. I like it when the kids tell us

complete joy like the perfection come to us
from high never fades. these children keep

us moving to the spot where Gabriel blows his
wondrous victory horn for the people of the

block.

[The Long Arm of Hate]

in the white church with the new
education wing more stiffly pressed

than a dress shirt back from the dry
cleaners, worshipers tuck ignorance

between the pages of brand new bibles,
and make faces at the brown skinned

guest speaker sharing facts schoolchildren
in an age of intolerance and hate learn

each day. in fevered eyes that held looks
of beating the colored man until fatigue

set in and cords turned red, the thought of
finding Christ was not better than picturing

a truth teller dead. many cannot hear stories
of hungry bellies around the corner from

the church, jaundiced drunks across the street
expiring on city park benches, refugees in flight,

violence in their cultural cracks, and the homeless
elderly Latino beaten to death by two white brothers

inspired by Trump rhetoric. the history of Black,
Brown, Yellow and Red dying, the battery, rape,

captivity, genocide, and hate is disallowed by
itchy-fists in this downtown worship place with

a very different use for God.

[Colors]

to be brown with a Spanish
speaking tongue in America
is to find doors locked, bitter
scorn, tearful sadness always
near. to be brown in America
is to have your working hands
turned inside out to slave, your
children shoved aside, barking
goose-steppers trampling with
boots the tiniest light of new
American dreams. to be brown
with a Spanish name in America is
clocking in to work for a sinfully
penny wage, to hear crooners on
the streets, in the schools, in front of
altar rails, on buses, trains and riding
in cars shout in your direction get out!
to be brown with a Spanglish speaking
tongue is to be told by citizens who suffer
a compassion disorder this place of birth
is exactly where you don't belong. I say
to be brown in America means conjuring the
words of the boy shot on the way to school
who declared with a stutter there is no land
of the free unless it speaks truthfully of the
picture that exists—a world of colors together
with me.

[The Moon]

why do we bother with the moon
surrounded by the stars that has

from the beginning inched away
from us? why sit on the cold steps to

look at the shadows so clearly made
by the gray disc, while Tito Puente plays

on a borrowed box? why do mothers
walk with strollers beneath her beams

spelling with chalk on the building walls
hope with every pause they happen to make?

why does the tree in the little park where
city sparrows perch to eat applaud when

they let the moonlight in? Why does this
orb in the sky make some bones cry and

lovers kiss? we look upon your shimmering
face to unlock the secrets of the soul you have

tirelessly gazed on earth with your dances
in the sky. you made in the darkness of

time tell us how long will frail humanity pan
the signs of life for righteous light?

[The School Visit]

this women with the broken eyebrows
made everything clear about her visit to

the public school where she had three kids
enrolled. she stares at me for a moment

with wide open eyes I imagine like a creature
in the woods unexpectedly caught by light,

then begins with the story of her home, the
man who didn't stay, the childhood games

she use to play, and the abominable public
school that makes her children feel like pariahs

each day. with tears rolling down her cheeks, she
tells me how she tried to banish Spanish every

evening in the home to help her children adapt
to this land where diversity is just another name

for more of the same, then she gasped for air turning
to the theme of her children in school treated like

their presence taints the classroom and stinks
the air. we walked the rest of the block together

and the women confessed to me that all she
really wants for her three kids is to hear them

say school is good, then see them grow inside this
life too many think belongs exclusively to them.

she turned the corner saying adios to make her way
to the school meeting leaving me to humbly ask what

now?

[My Love]

my love is on the streets with the poor
who have names only God in this city

can conjure up. when the wind
pushes against their windows on the

last floor of the slack building without
a number on its front door, I love to talk

with them till dawn about the angry Lord
who raises storms on the greedy streets of

the prosperous flock downtown. I love the way
abuela rolls her eyes at the church bells that

ring to chase the twisted angels in the building
down the street to the subway and back to

the furthest place from the weak. I love to
hear the stories the mother's tell of walking

the shores of a restless sea finding peace
laid in the sand in a speckled shell, how

they make rumors about the moon, the sky,
the stars, and the breezes caressing their blistered

hands. you will not find beautifully bound
books tell sopping tales like those of men,

women and children who speak on this block
like spies of paradise lost. I love to hear them

say one day soon the poor will see sadness in
this land wrapped with the amnesty the young

priest says has come.

[The Stroll]

I would like to stroll down the
street talking about the light

in others keeping the block from
the uncertain dark, describing the

simplest joys of the mothers in the
little park, reaching for the clocks

that resemble frightened rabbits on
the run to stop them in return for

tenderness to wake on the corners
of the world. I would like to stand

beneath the leaning trees with birds
pick up a handful of them to closely

watch them sing of flight around the
old tenements, rest on the fire escapes,

and above our Spanish speaking children's
heads. I would like to think of bread on

a table shared by the Cruz family without
a tear shed, of milk for Ana's two young

girls, and the block dazed with the most
wonderful touches of love. I would like to

walk past the church to talk with the most
blessed about my last conversation with the

dead who said pray us up from the dust.

[The Television]

do you know how to step into a new world?
Shorty said it is the easiest thing to do just

turn on the television on any night of the week
to see the thousands of different ways you do

not live, the countless worlds that will never
send you a thing, the dread feeling there is

no place for you here. I watched those shows
raising all kinds of wishful dreams to help me

dance across another day praising the little
light coming into my dark living room, full of all

kinds of words to throw at the images on the T.V.
screen. I saw friends turn into blood puddles

on the sidewalk corner no one talked about on
the evening news save to name the many ways

the billionaires debate the cost of vintage rum
and remain oblivious to how their thoughts feed it.

Shorty prefers to watch the young full moon when
it hangs over the roof of his building where he spends

the Summer days flying kites, he loves to call the sky
holding it the picture frame of his American dream, since

it brings the biggest smiles to his mother's tired face.
I ran into Shorty one afternoon on the way home from

public school sixty-six told him television is full
of a whole lot of experts telling you how to make

your raggedy clothes clean—pointless, man.
we walked home together, silently. then, Shorty

turning to the steps of his building shouted we
need a show about the people life cheats.

[The Watch Fixer]

when we took the apartment an old
Jewish man was living on the ground

floor who kept an open window with
a sign above it that read watch repair

shop. I saw darkness crumble every
time a watch that had collected a little

dust was left for him to bring back to
life. the world was motionless on the table

with so many parts small enough to
fit in a tear, his gentle eyes were

covered by thick magnified specs I told
him one morning could see the world

awake before clock alarms made noise, and
it made him chuckle. one summer morning

we sat watching the city sun come up, he told
me watches break some times by a fall and strangely

the motion of trains, their guts pushed to silence,
but these things can be fixed with the busy labor of

wrinkled hands. the grace I came to know on the
block was given by this old Jewish man's simple

lesson about the value of broke things helped to
mend.

[Rice Rain]

mothers on the block told me one
late Spring it rained rice, there were no

screams on any of the corners, old women
danced on the street, and fine-looking birds

rested on the telephone wires catching
the grains. I thought they were disguising

difficult times with made up things that
no one in the rest of the world could find

a way to believe. I listened to their stories
spilling into the day noticing how the chatter

of woe on Simpson Street withdrew to grant
us a bigger slice of gladness. I carry them

with me now across every season, seconds in
a day, whenever darkness digs into my soul,

much like the secrets stars keep. I never saw
the miracle they described with my own two eyes.

so I keep myself prepared without a trace of misgiving
for rice rain to pour some day from clouds to gently

wake an incredulous world awake to better things.

[There you Stand]

I see you full of life standing in front of me
telling me in Spanish of a hope that feeds you

and lets you hold with certainty heaven
in your palm. the sounds coming out of

your mouth are hauled around town by your
mother, found in the suitcase your father

packed twenty-five years ago for a long
walk away from home, on your sister's lips

when she sings in the storefront church, riding on
the subway at rush hour holding on to Jesus straps

complaining of a lifetime of factory work, pouring
out of the children who stay after school for English

lessons they will recall deleting their names, and from
the grandmothers made of Spanish, your voice

with flooded pleas rises to say do not forget the native
soil mothers left behind, or go missing from birth,

or turn away from the sentiments of Spanish in this
new land lived. I see you standing in front of me in the

hungry sounds of Victor's four sisters who stare at last
night's crumbs on the kitchen table wondering about their

next full meal, in the back alley shouting at the windows
for someone to drop petty change for food, insisting with the

most moving *palabras* not to allow the world that despises
spics to damage our dreams.

[Saturday Night Confession]

what time does confession start
so I can tell the priest about the
victims of my behavior like sneaking

in to the movies without paying, praying
on one knee in church, jumping over the
turnstile to catch a subway ride, dropping

lies the size of Leroy's building about
never missing a day of school, and taking
a loan of a few bucks from Saint Joseph

who stood motionless on the family altar
of a less than perfect home? what time
does our neighborhood religious leader

who speaks with a twisted angels voice
show up to listen to the stories of cursing,
fights, muddled bible reading, and all the

dope shooting that helps us strike it poor?
I heard last week Lelo spilled himself in
the confessional then said a bunch of

prayers at the altar rail to clear himself
with heaven even though Father Smith
told his favorite altar boy he had trouble

hearing a thing that was said. when I entered
the confessional asking Father when will I hear
the voice that said let there be light, the one that

makes the blind see, the limp run, and raised
Lazarus from the dead? the answer I got was say five
our fathers and ten hail Mary's, so I wondered who

the hell was forgiving God for the sin of not
ever bothering to show up.

[Waiting]

once again you sat the long night with
me turning the pages of a book of dreams,

experiencing the mysterious ways the dark
endured beat against the stoop steps. I see you

under the vagrant stars, the words departing sweetly
from your lips, moments of tender laughter shared

on the deserted steps, and the new day naked to life is
continuously beautiful, again. I marked the crack on the

step where you use to sit knowing well it would still be there
after years of walking in the English speaking wilderness.

yesterday, I waited for you on that very spot imagining
you were not so far, and when you did not come I placed

a flower on the stoop for the wind somehow to carry to
your sweet missing lips. one day, I will return to take you

by the hand that makes the clocks go back to thank you
for teaching me how to let love in without a need for

words.

[The Pew]

I sat in the pew listening to a man
reading from a xenophobic bible with

rubbish about a God who does not make
colorful things, the hills green, the night

black, the day bright, nature alight with
difference, speech for many different tongues

and a world with no dividing walls to jump.
for years I haven't cried with my face in my

hands in a sanctuary serving sham stories of
the divine. the stranger who works weekly for

the church clearing the lawn of weeds is the
person the errant bible reader should seek when sitting

alone in chapel, or awake at night disturbed, for
in the stranger's face is the purest glimpse of all

holy things. I prayed for him to bend
his knees, keep an eye out for the angels circling

above his foolish head, and listen closely to the
words of love spoke by his dark skinned savior

king who never sat on a white throne and shouted
for release at Golgotha in the company of two other

crucified Jews.

[The Politician]

there is a politician leaning over
us like a trained guard dog snapping
on his chains, eager to pound widows
and orphans to dust, waiting to push
us over the border, happy to make
the earth spin with us dead on it. on
the last day of the world, he would still
draw us into the terrible womb of the
worlds filthiest rot, and before anyone
dared speak a word this politician would
declare himself with urgency everlasting
king. is anyone asking in the cocktailed
dinner parties, the lavish ballrooms, and the
democratic chambers, what good will come
with the likes of him? hell has more doors
than this nation states, and now a wicked
politician to walk us in.

[The Convention]

I must go to place with the liberty bell
around which hope gathers in the warm

hearts that ooze multicolored dreams. I
must go to that place freedom works in the

brightened lips of people who spell America
without ignorance spread, who live with the

memory of what was done and what will come
ahead, who speak in countless tongues. I must

climb to the highest hill where the deepest founding
vision rests, catch my breath in the silence, and

in the wordless moment let my beloved America
with her colors sink deeply in me.

[Forgotten Civil War]

I searched on all the streets to find
a place where the sharp knife of grief

was not at work making hope drift
like wood tossed to sea. I stopped on

West Farms Road to find this fleeting
friend in the old hands of Teresa who

sat on the steps with her long black hair
scattered around her face by the breeze, she

knows this earth in Spanish with love too
thin to speak. she told me she sits on the

steps everyday waiting for the dreamy play
of life on the block to end and angels to fall

from the sky proclaiming do not be afraid.
In the palm of her left hand Teresa held a

wedding band that reminded her of vows whispered
on a foothill in a land far away in front of witnesses

who dreamed of another life with the smell of
gun-powder lingering in their lungs. two unsuspecting

children walk past, with a smile she reaches out to
them, then with words that cling to memories of loss

from the flight North, the old woman parts the curtain
of her heart a little more and looks at me quietly saying

one day a new start with magnificent hope and kindness
will rise from the ashes of torturers to bring us complete

peace.

[Soul]

my soul is restless under the influence
of moonlight, wandering where all thoughts

in a dark space live and look carefully for a
window with light. it summons thousands

of years back with unsuspecting ethereal
reach for ancestral origin and watches the

living torn by loneliness, indifference, hate
and time that brims with strife. my soul in the

name of those who have silently died and turn
up in dreams, admits seasons of madness drown

the living with deficient forms of peace. my soul
is tired of bandaging the wounded who wait for heavens

glories to come to feel life complete. when I shut my
eyes does it find a field with flowers or just weeds

withering in the dark? in the mysterious vastness
will it drift long on the currents between light and

blackness unanswerable to the world? my soul
overflows into the corners of my mind where the

mumbled divine name is expected to answer to
the cries and pounding on the walls that ask it to

descend to kindly look upon everything to be
bettered and thoroughly changed.

[The Opera]

the opera made the night famous
for the cities high culture class who

drove to it on streets named after men
who gave a final curtain call no doubt

believing their last breath would deliver
them to Jacob's ladder. the Marquis of Mambo

who was also the Opera House custodian, living
on Avenue D, would not attend the show

in spite of hours laboring to clean the place
for those to applaud the tenor who can hold

Bizet's longest notes and Carmen in her lacy
black dress and eyes wide open with tragedy.

the opera crowd will laugh, cry, and see the
world differently with smiles on their faces

for the well performed grim tale of Seville. the
custodian thinks after the show, the wrecked

theater goers should visit Thompkins Square
Park on Avenue C to find the real Carmen who

sleeps on a bench covering her body with the
city paper. they should deliver to this woman

a Red rose wreath for finding food to eat each
long day—*excusez-moi* Bizet this Carmen let

no one forget!

[First Day of School]

it happened in public school sixty-six the
morning of the first day of class, Miriam

tripped over her words the whole long
day for speaking only Spanish. she came

home in tears promising to have answers for
the teacher the next day when asked what did

you do this Summer, so she began to rehearse
lines from the Dick and Jane library book that

had gathered dust for three months in the corner
of her room, then she played an Aretha Franklyn

song the one called Think and memorized the
verse you better think about what you are

doing to me to pitch to her teacher to let her
feel what it's like to trip on words. she spent

the night practicing English determined not to
let the school pull her Spanish mouth out for the

rubbish bin that oddly the Puerto Rican custodian
emptied at the end of the school day with his Spanish

speaking hands. from that day on she embraced the
bitter and the sweet and told her teachers in America

the Spanish she speaks to talk at home, pray to God,
and even dream is protected by the constitution right

called freedom of speech.

[I Take Your Hand]

let me take your hand before
they come for us at dawn

to walk us past the holy candles
burning for all the families from

villages stained by revolutionary
blood. let me take your hand before

you die on this New York street so far
from the hills you always tell me the ancient

shepherd loves, for you to have time to cry
about the lost evenings swinging in a hammock

on the vestibule of the home your unschooled
father built in the middle of a civil war with

his own sweat, and your mother blessed each
Easter with holy water collected at the entrance

of the Cathedral of the poor. let me take your
hand before the sidewalk turns into a shadow

that makes people hoping to live disappear in the
dark. I promise to hold your hand tightly, kneel

in candid prayer and hand you a new lighted candle
to lead you beyond the buildings that shout curses to

heaven toward the one corner on the block that
offers unimagined tenderness for cruelly bent

hearts.

[The Valley]

once in the valley I met an old
woman sitting on the road oddly
in a pool of tears. for many years
she mixed her sorrow with the rain
to make this curious puddle for those
now gone. since the civil war's end
she discomforted by life has said very
little with her fragile tongue to people
going about their business. I sat with her
trying to feed love to her broken heart, adding
my own tears to the murky pool, and plummeting
to the places in her death touched. when silence
overcame us I was nagged by the need to find
answers to my questions about why life for her so
bent? how would she reach the sweet people taken
from this earth? when no reply came back, I admitted
this is what passing through the world sometimes does,
then I reached to take her hand, and strangely she floated
away before my very eyes responsive only to the wind.

[Lost and Found]

how sad are the days gone
that will never come back
to these streets where once
the children played in fire
hydrant water with wet bare
feet. how sad the distant past
that in a timeless tomb keeps the
voices we live to forget. how
sad the empty lots with apartments
left alone never to be touched. how
sad to live in a time that refuses to
let the voices that feed the earth
in. how sad to inhale a world
so far from what is needed and
to forget the wisdom that says
we will never lose our way. how
sad not to understand one fresh day
this city like Jerusalem delivered.

[Mission]

returning home you will search for these
kids in the simple things not far from where
the distance crumbled when you took them by
the hand in a simple dusty school. search for them
in the birds at play, the birds hopping on the branches
of trees, the laughter of the evening wind, the blue
sky that makes the weeping still, the pictures you
will dream, the prayers you will recite to give magnificent
life for them. search for these children in the words to spill
from your lips, in their innocent love that will forever
look upon your face, in every prayer to heaven you
make that settles on the throne so near to the forgotten
and the weak. search for them in your times of silence,
acts of kindness and whenever you magically hear them
whispering across the distance tenderly in your ears.

[The Post Office]

I hadn't noticed until stopping,
the lines at the post office are
longer than the stone faces of
its clerks. the guy in front of
me holding letters with addresses
for delivery across the border was
on it long enough to receive visitors,
one elderly woman said since May,
and the mother with her restless kids
holding several packages was certain
it would not move sooner than the universe
would end. I could hear the mail clerks
asking customers looking straight
at them how soon do you want the
package delivered with a look in their
eyes already counting the days, and
the old woman with a cloud above her
tired head replying dearest before I
expire.

[When the Angels Come]

I have nothing to give you except
care on this sidewalk of the church

the priest leads afraid to say a word
about the end of exploitation. I can

listen to the world beside you making
the long walk that keeps you looking to

heaven waiting for a star to fall into
your arms with answers to everything.

I can share with you stories of a great
love that with unreserved innocence cast

its influence further than the imaginings
of power will ever reach. I will help you

build a house of rest pleasing to the one
who wears a thorn crown to gather in its

chambers the people cracked by work for
small coins, without a thrill for saintly books,

and disbelieving the soon and very soon the
hallelujahs constantly sing. I will be on all the

corners with you until the angels come to lift us
up with their wings

[Holy Night]

at this moment, the street light went out
and the scavenging dog begins to bark,

no doubt concerned about being left to
search in the dark. a boy is standing below

an open window looking up using his voice
like a car horn to yell for his friend Angel

to come downstairs I suspect to walk over
to the block party on Fox Street where the

obscure Bronx world is sung. leaning on
the fire hydrant near the middle of the block

Hank whose fingers have not held another
hand for years lifts a pint bottle of Midnight

Express sips the pure alcohol disguised like
wine then smiling remarks to strollers *I think*

this is heaven. along comes the leader of the
storefront church certain his great God has

not filled the wino with a single drop of grace,
but Tito's mother who brings the tortured soul

a cup of rice with a simple act of kindness says
that cannot be true. right now, Hank eats and

converses with the invisible Great Being who
moves the moon, stars, air, earth and people

like him from the fringes to the Saints—to
this I say Amen!

[The Living Room]

there you are in grandmother's apartment
listening to music that crossed into the

living room from another time, shuffling
a deck of cards to amuse yourself, with your

caged memories spilled loose on crumbled
paper scattered around the dark room floor.

once again you retreated to your favorite
place to watch the world pass by in Spanish

in the songs your grandmother taught you to
sing from records stored in a big box. you

pull me into the dark living room to say a
a different America lives inside of us just

look at the old men sitting in front of the bodega
heaving Spanish carved from the scars on their heads

at the English speaking day, walk down third avenue
to see Sparrows hopping the sidewalks do not tweet

a single Americano word, and the uptown life needing
an English speaking God to worship is worthless here

on the block. I sit with you recalling a time our wallets burst
with emptiness and we found broken English jobs packing

coats into boxes eight floors above Seventh Avenue
until downtown crowds parted. now, I see like a blind

man reading braille what you mean it is difficult to find
patience inside a city of parched wells.

[The Disappeared]

the disappeared are now remembered
in the tattered news print kept in a shoe
box by a mother who has slipped into the
corners of less to say. the important days
too are disappearing into the barren spaces
of her heart that evil keeps from finding
peace. she hears her daughter's voice at night
lunging from the shadows, walking through
the noise of the market place, the back of
the church when the priest forgets to lift the
child up in prayer, the frail memories of days
together that now in this dreadful time of absence
accuse the authors of war of taking the innocent
away. a bitter wind always blows in this mother's
face who at night is awakened by dreams of bones rattling
alone in the ground crying the words help me. in her
kitchen with goblets filled with tears the mother pleads
to heaven with a soul already lying in her child's most
certain grave. every morning she makes her way
to the neighborhood church to light candles to the Mother
of Peace to pray the girl disappeared is not still in sleep
and one day wandering the world will come home.

[Once A Wish]

I once had a wish to see dew formed on an early morning sidewalk never raked, to see flowers pushing through concrete cracks instead of rotting like waste, to listen to doves wakening the day for the tired who never turned back to the villages they left. I once had a wish to see souls fly over the little park when the congas played at twilight, to hear on this earth the sounds of the ones who left us draw close from the distance, to see the planets turning without explanation. I once had a wish to see the crowded church around the corner drop its heavenly script in favor of lifting hearts for tender love on the streets, to see the hated junkies become the face of God, to see life on the block bond to so much dust find the light illuminating a sign that reads almost there. I once had a wish to find the good Lord roaming about the heavenly garden dispensing clear thoughts in simple speech to quench the thirst for words that help us make sense of pitiless time here—perhaps, someday with a flash of presto magic these wishes will come true.

[Homeless]

the boy with the hoarse voice tried to
evict the idea he was lost, in a river
being washed to sea, and plunging into
a hole that eats dreams. at midnight,
the wind hitting the chimes hanging on
Marta's fire escape window made him
play at being loved on the dark and lonely
street. his homeless body slouched in the
shadows of the tenement steps with cardboard
for a bed, bleak in the morning sun, cold
in the loneliness of night fear, tearful in
every feeble attempt at prayer, is an innocent
heart that feels. who's to blame for this child's
nights beneath shivering stars and his flattening
days? How could a mother withdraw love and a
father run from reach? how long till the people
passing on the street begin to curse his aches?
the boy with the hoarse voice wondered the last
time he visited St. John's Chrysostom church
where an old priest once poured water on his infant
head what happened to merciful love—gone for kids
like him.

[New Shoes]

my brother's new shoes rest at the
foot of his bed. after three weeks of

shining shoes on the boulevard with his
bony hands to buy them he has fallen in

love with these new covers for his feet. I can
see they are perfect, stainless, shiny enough

to catch even the tiniest light in the room, ready
for two small feet to hurry out the door, and up the

street glimmering like black pearls. he plans to
wear them to Easter Mass with a pair of ten-percent

silk pants and a multicolored Alpaca sweater he
found in somebody's trash. every night he falls out

of his heart looking at those shoes, and I gently tease
every time they hurry around the apartment, up the street

or kneel at the altar rail. he wears them to listen to
the world feeling a joy unexplained by the priest, though

I am certain it has something to do with his dreams. I
cannot look at a new pair of shoes now without waving

a candle to the stars deep in my heart, then smile ever
so big.

[Lead Me]

she led me by the hand across the
street to the place where the last
tears fell for people who believe
nothing changes. I stood on that
spot with her taking in the sounds
of the morning, lost for words and
certain not even the busy wind would
find the simplest confession of any
interest. I imagine what it must have
been like to let those tears go, to have
faith they are received somewhere in
a heaven that hangs above the moon,
and touch the lips of the Great mute
she claims walks these very streets.
I wanted to surrender to her faith, to
feel my bones take the same shape,
to forget the thousands of times the
three mothers with deceased kids have
said the good Lord roams this block
forgetting. quietly, I listened to this
non-bearded messenger who yet held
my hand recite Spanish prayers for the
descendants of the block living in a
world of screams and waiting meekly
for prayers to be fulfilled.

[The Chevy]

when the burnt orange 1957 Chevy
Junior fixed up with wheels more

expensive than his weekly pay check
drove past, the mid-afternoon monotony

of the block was flung from every head
that turned to get a look. he loved to park

that thing wherever the wind was still and
the poor kids were certain not to play tag

around its fins. before his daughter was
fully grown she learned to sit tightly for fast

rides on a public road used for a quarter mile
race strip, while all the jealous kids on the block

swore the little papa's girl could fly. no one
could climb into that car without conjuring

hundreds of ways to toss visions from its racing
light to strangers on the street. whenever that

overdone car drove by the people on the block
found the remade metal Pegasus crushed the

bitterness in them. one very wet day Junior
cruised by the bodega when Sonia was leaving

it with a brown bag filled with thirty-five cents
of dinner herbs and she declared out loud with

a most exquisitely radiant look on her face one
day I will drive a car like that to other worlds,

delicious, sweet and true.

[Awake]

I watched the slow door of the elementary
school open in a silent dream with thirsting
children run out expecting to find paradise
weeping into the blackest corners of their
day. I counted their round faces filled with
hope that soared higher than the pigeons could
fly and heard the sounds of their love press
against the sharp-edged world. on this day,
a teacher filed out behind them, his name
and history the children knew, the happy
mothers who had learned to tell time by the
sound of their children's hearts were on their
way a block away, and mystery floated on the
gray cement sidewalk different from the way
priests taught it. I looked up to see the sky
unsure of its light and awakened giving thanks
for the poor on a block that has the best year round
view of innocent love.

[A Mother Gone]

in the pouring rain I woke up
suddenly thinking about the

people in the apartment below
and the night the sirens howled

to the front steps of the building
and the medics carted away the

crack head mother with two bony
children. I heard the two kids with

complicated lives crying when the
bitter night with its sad Angels collided

with their heads. these two grew up after
that night mostly on the corner never facing

home and always looking down the street
to the window where the grandmother who

came to them singing leaned out nights to
keep watch. on another cold night sirens again

awakened me and I thought of the times I saw
the old lady looking over the dark streets, watching

tired old men reading newspapers on the stoop, and
chatting it up with number runners. when the

bedroom clock announced it was a quarter to three,
I planned to ask this old lady what do you see from

the window? If she stiffened her neck, I vowed
to press the question can you return the mothers

who have left?

[Morning]

in the busy sounds of the summer morning
in the city the greyish faces on the sidewalk

look like wickless candles disturbed for a new day,
the hot dog carts roll to the corners while small

birds fly about them, shops undo their noisy gates,
and a parade of suits marches in step along the

avenue to the discordant cries of beggars taking
their spots. the colors of the day could not be more

perfect to set the people going like low-cost working
clocks. the morning talk shuffles along with all the

holy hush that nonsense topics give, and the Utmost
in the clear blue sky once again with silence says

enjoy the paradise. today, I suspect the stuttering
steps recall precisely how heaven was brought to us—so

why not enjoy the morning air!

[The Refugee Woman]

pause in front of the apartment door,
where the woman who packed a life

in a suitcase waited years to be born
again on this blood soaked earth. stand

on the building steps to get a good look
at the people who dwell across the street

who gave her bread to settle the pounding
poverty in her home. stop to have a talk

with her to harvest memories of loss, the
vanished mouths of her dearest dead, the

insane divinity that comes inflicting pain.
listen to her speak in the half-dark chamber

of apartment 5-C of the low voices that still
cry out from the abscessing inhumanity of the

country she fled. when her tired hands offer
you a glass of water for stopping in to see her,

all dressed up in black tears, walk down the street,
feel her weight in your veins, and throw your

light back to her deepest wishes.

[Store Front Church]

I heard singing coming from the store front
church, felt its spell fill haunted spots on the

block, and saw sunken souls ascend the
dark with peace. I went to the rooftop looked

at the vivid sky of stars and shouted for a sign
from above to swiftly bend nearer to us. I

could hear tambourines, earnest cries, and the
Pentecostal preacher's simple prayers for the

the feverish sacred light to shine upon the pale
lives in need. I sat quietly thinking about when

a few nights earlier the city loosened shadowy hands
to rattle the gutter sleepers to their feet and that same

store front man of God made notes to climb into
a pulpit with a pack of words rolling from his dusty

lips. when sleep finally came I wanted to know had
anyone ever seen a messenger with wings, the face

of Jesus on the street or a troublemaking serpent in the
little park's trees? quickly, I realized it's the secret of

the questions that please me so I took a moment to say
a little prayer myself begging for the Spirit that makes

us fearless to come, unveiled.

[They Came]

we sat on your father's veranda
and talked about the day the soldiers
came marching down the long hill
kicking stones lying on the ground
along the way. the uniforms were
buttoned tight and their boots were
still stained from the last campaign in
the neighborhood that after all these years
is remembered to be the place where youth
was quickly snuffed. the day the men
came to make us lay in graves with trick
questions still digs too deep into the world
of our thumping hearts. we talked about
carrying that day far enough into another
life for the haunting to stop and smiling
wide when that moment comes, since it will
be more precious than all the flowers in this
world.

[The Night Club Shooting]

in my heart that wails today with
the names of those never known in
the lightless dark of other hate, I wish
to tell you with the clenched fist of the
witnesses, the broken spirit of friends,
the hollering pain of family, the violence
of decapitated Islam must end.

unspeakable feelings now slide forward in
disquieting questions: what has gay humanity
done to anger the nightclub killer's gun? what
God washed humanity from the evil man's
twisted head? who wrapped his soul in chains
to deafen him to love, kindness and truth?

in the tragic tunnel dark, we are left now
to walk with tears, answers to our questions
may never come, yet those of us preparing
the burials ahead will reminisce the departed
imagining their sweet moments, their gentle first
kiss, how they cradled feelings of belonging, and

confidently embraced their divine blessings without
end. I have no doubt lightless hearts and hands stained
with murderous blood are bound to the devil-himself
who will collect from the likes of this felonious scum
the fullest never-ending fare.

[The Window View]

I once lived in an apartment high enough
to see the east river from the living room

window. the circle line boat would push
north along the water way with tourists on

board I imagined saying unbelievable things
with the setting sun above them faintly warming

like a declining fire. on the walls of the Brooklyn
shore I could see spray painted colors with messages

from the homeboys on the other side, and hiding in
some bushes beneath a plastic tarp, the figure of

a man sitting on the bank like a loose thread about
to unravel the secrets of Mark Twain's river stories,

nodding his head. once when night dropped, I heard
the restless voices I love rising from the dark river, up

beyond the tenement top floor apartments, wandering
in the clouds and whispering come hither to find rest.

I never found the right words to describe the feelings
these voices ever so clearly delivered to me from the

rivers steady swift currents, yet like a pleasant dream
in a season of sadness I swore the whole earth spoke to

me.

[June Morning]

down by the noisy lake I did meet
with broken friends to seek what

God has to say to us who tremble
with grief. now with the screaming

still, those we will lower into graves
to slide into the world of ancient dust

make our mortal hearts wish to hear a
single word of hope from your sacred

lips. we prayed for friends who will no
longer walk the earth, know love pouring

from their hearts, talk the sidewalk cafes
into the late night, and embrace quarreling

companions with adoring gestures of love.
we passed pictures around of breathless

faces for whom to pray with heaven-seeking
eyes filled with hardened tears. begin now

divine Spirit to speak, tell us what you think,
do not leave us helpless in the world's punishing

state, you know what the killer did, tell us
in paradise he shall not live.

[In Memory]

the night sometimes proposes to
eat us without a sole revelation
shuddering toward our wide open
eyes. the tender moon cannot keep
it from making the rounds to collect
victims for the end and leaving some of
us behind to weep. the morning death
carriages play the songs that tighten
around our hearts while we march
like the wind to the burial grounds to
say good-bye to those who were happy
in their days to merely be loved. mother
of God in this mad world burning blameless
life like the furious sun when will evil end?
wherever you are today wipe away the sadness
in us and gives us hope with your best simplest
speech.

[The Caged Bird]

my mother won a Parakeet on a
ten cent spin of a numbered wheel

hanging on plywood at the cheapest
amusement park in town. the bird

came with a cage and it made mother
sing more merrily than her new winged

friend who every now and then whistled
the bird version of Bronx truth. we

got the Parakeet in the cage home,
placed it in the living room with the name

of a famous Mexican revolutionary, and
every time she lost a cheap factory job

you could find her sitting on a rocker she
got for Mother's Day talking the bird to

sleep. My God—the bird knew a great deal
more about the troubling in her soul and the

strange faith that kept her going than any of
her kids, friends or the confessional priest.

on restless nights, I could hear her in the
living room speaking Spanish to her little

Pancho Villa who was always willing to carry
the appalling blasphemies of life kicking up

the dust knocking on her door. one night
I heard her drinking tears, the concerned bird

was skipping in the cage, and a surprising clarity
made me understand there will always be a voice

speaking Spanish in the dark.

[The Blessing Box]

when the bus did not come he
began to iron crumbled paper
carried to his feet by air, a few

yards away a swarm of kids talking
loud pitched pennies against fat Isaac's
tenement, and the scene for some unexplained

reason made him reflect on the small rectangular
cases fixed to the front doors of apartments in the
building with Torah text inside. the Jewish super

called these rectangular things the box that protects
the Mezuzah or piece of Torah scroll intended to bring
blessings to Jewish homes. he looked down the street

again for the bus, scratched his head and thought
surely these blessing boxes must stand guard just the
same over my mother living in fat Isaac's building.

the bus still did not come, the bodega owner rolled
down the metal gate protecting stuff in his shop, and
the penny pitching crowd had already left. as it grew

darker with no bus in sight, he thought the good Lord
on this earth is one of us, struggling to make the
rent, finding worldly worth just standing quietly on

fat Isaac's rooftop enjoying the stars, thankful for a
stomach full of rice and dreaming up new words to tell
of saving grace—finally the bus pulled up and he gladly

rolled away!

[The Poet's Street]

it was dark on Longfellow Avenue
named after the Maine poet who liked
the quiet spirit in the woods strolling
over the moss-grown stones to the places
with white flowers in bloom. with a strong
back Victor sat every night on a long bench
placed in his living room to think of this fragile
street become a bottomless pit for collecting
the aging sentiments running down so many tired
cheeks. the people he comes from never heard
of Longfellow, their buried dead built the bridge
that carried Victor to the block, and on unbearable
days they make up songs Longfellow never dreamed.
one day on the subway ride to work he stumbled on
an article featuring the New England poet, so when
he got home to his long bench picturing what he would
say to his new friend—Longfellow remove your shoes,
forget the woods with flowering trees, shoot your
arrows into the air, and breathe new songs wherever
you are with me for the people living on your aching
city street.

[Absent Father]

with you the word was not flesh
the day children were born in the city

hospital that welcomed the newest
infant you fathered into the divided

light. we never heard you say your
name, pose for a photo in the apartment

we lived, gather love for us when all the
rooms in the house were choked with

strife, or breathe life into the aching
hearts of your three kids. you disappeared

one night leaving us to sleep in a shared
bed the neighbors said was made from

the bones of the dead. after many years
silent you learned your oldest son had buckled

over dead on a desolate sidewalk on a rainy
night in the Bronx, the news did not rush you

to his sad grave. our trembling souls followed
the southern shores to reach you living in the

rice fields at the foot of the Andes mountains
with the hidden news only to return to the stoop

flooding those who grieved with the darkest thoughts.
one late night hour, I went to the church swallowing

our tears to be filled with that gracious love that watches
over unopened flowers to find the courage that would

allow me never again to call you father—the greater light
you see made you just another man who burnt precious

hours without tender love and tears.

[The Refugee Family]

in the evening the night rang with
deadly guns shipped from the north
to soldiers hands no longer going

without food to eat. for hours the
air turned black with smoked earth
kicked up by the five-hundred pound

bombs dropped on village heads by
men taking orders from others who
had no love to give. what was this

civil war? a huge festering infection
of common life, faces of catechists
skinned to the bone, death running

loose with the vigor of youth in the
coffee fields, village squares, holy
churches and terrified hearts. you can

find our country on a map sitting quietly
in a library chair without ever knowing
it was a land of an inhumane plague where

God was even made a partner of the ugly work
of the owners of the earth. we fled north with
the guns still rattling death at our heels, came to

this land that disbelieved our refugee pleas, told
us we came to steal its daily bread, and never stopped
spending millions of dollars to see us killed. at night,

I think of my decapitated friends with the chilling
voice of the governor playing in the back of my
head who says people like us must leave. the Lord's

Prayer often tightens around my throat to make
me cough words in my mother tongue that in simple
English say: give us this day our daily bread and deliver

us from the wicked indifference of politicians who
never see the world with eyes like us.

[The First Poem]

my little girl sat down tonight
to write the sweetest lines with
a few words bigger than she could
say. she sat in front of my favorite
old wood desk pressing words to a
screen, every now and then turning
to toss a smile in the direction of the
study window with the faint scratching
of the tiny green lizard who has made
a good backyard friend. when I asked
about her writing with eager eyes and a
gentle smile she said, "Daddy please do
not distract me." the darling night will
not know a more beautiful time than this
moment with heaven so near in the pint-size
verse you worked to share with mother, brother
and me. my sweet girl, you already know how
to make the stubborn dark fall and how to
find your soul in Eden—write the years you
grow and never ever stop.

[The Waiting Room]

on the Lower East Side I went to
the hospital at 2 a.m. to sit in the

waiting room with Carlos who was
sitting in the pits with folded hands

absorbed by the news of his sister's
spoiled heart. he was staring at the double

doors across the room waiting for the doctor
to appear shouting his name with the latest. he

was visibly lost in that haunted waiting space
visited frequently by nurses who wore shallow

smiles to trim with tenderness news they preferred
not to speak. we talked till the rising sun about a

prayer sister Emilia wrote in broken English for
the children of the Aquila family born on Avenue D,

the African violets blooming in his kitchen and how
his sister loved to sit beside them pronouncing the plain

honest truth of life. he shared with me the names
of the immortal songs he adored in the hymnals lifting

madness with wings, the questions arising within about
the unseen mysteries they sing, and how he wished one

of them would shout a healing for sweet leaking heart
at dawn, the doctor walked into the waiting room

alone with a mask pulled below his chin to tell Carlos
the end was near. I stroked the back of his hand, looked

into his swollen eyes, and promised together we would
find our way.

[So far Away]

never in a dream did I think home
too far away for the history books

to note with thirsty words. there
are people in that place with heads

full of stories told best by the old who
know by name everyone who carries

the sky to keep an eagle eye view
of passing life. I made a note of the

haunting faces of the poor to hold them
dear, the homes that have vanished so

many years ago, and the broken hearts
once comforted by the dark corners of the

night. I have known the warm embrace of
workers arms that picked coffee for pennies

all day, the stone faces of the harlots with
kids who played with me, and nights come

with street music to give wrecked families
peace. with certainty at different hours of

the day, I will tell you home is a strange
feeling gasping for air and leaning toward

tiny specks of light. rush down to this far
away place to let your crowded head clear

to the sound of prayers spoke in the dark,
and you will know exactly what I mean.

[Still Night]

the earth turns for the common folk
who can see naked names floating in

uneven days. beneath their eye lids
is the soul's deepest affliction, made

by the violence one bitter night in a
nightclub that twisted hearts into mounds

of discolored life. you can hear the talk
of ruin everywhere and the piety the disfiguring

evening dissolves easily now on tongues. in
the dark, we reach around blindly for light

to police the violent madness of hateful
men who see no crime in taking lives over

matters of difference. in the crying rooms, we
admit to living afraid without those who are now

forever gone. with gaping wounds, we plead for
God to listen to the whispers of our dead who from

the grave demand an end to hellish bleeding in
this world.

[Independence Day]

the subway conductors still talk about
the twelve kids who boarded the number
six train bound for Canal Street the Friday
before independence day to buy fire works
in China Town.

little Johnny who lived on the block worked
for the city on the subway line and knew every
one of those kids from the shoe shine corner on
the boulevard and that night he caught them writing
their names on the last car of his train.

the boys rushed in the city's brightness downtown,
convinced the inventors of gunpowder must have a
hush-hush shop on Mott Street for kids like them who
love to pledge allegiance to the flag throwing illicit
firecrackers on the streets.

the twelve gathered their shoe shine money into Rudy's
black beaver hat that was combed with baby oil for an
hour in anticipation of the great market venture—thirty-eight
dollars collected! they exited the subway on Canal Street
with the morning near spent, looked in all directions for a spot

to make the purchase—but nothing! the boys could not find
a store with smoke oozing from its doors, just the Kam Man
Food market with its assortment of teas, duck, pork, chicken,
and figurines of a chubby Buddha making all the scenes. then,
they noticed a hunched man on a park bench who looked

knowledgeable enough about those things not one of them
had ever actually seen in China Town, so they walked over
to ask—again, nothing! on the long ride back to the Bronx,
the aging shoe shine boys redistributed the funds, joked about
their qualms and planned to have a little flan on the block at

Junior's restaurant. funny, on the noisy 4th of July not one of these
boys whined, since joy was in their pockets made by a whole
lot of rattling coins not spent downtown for things that go boom!

[Holding Hands]

let me take your hand cutter of
cane, picker of corn, carrier of
coffee beans, shepherd of the
fields, sweeper of floors, keeper
of children, child of the street, and
mother of tears. let me walk with
you hearing everything into the
dark night until you no longer have
words left for sorrow. let me hold
you on the dusty paths of the world
toppling the memories of places you
were sadly punished, where children
no longer play, and the days pressed
your soul into hidden dungeons with
lock and lost keys. let me hold your
hand on the way to the mountain top
shadowed by your grace, past the
stony Sunday faces, along the trail with
moldering leaves beneath our tired feet,
to find in quiet silence deep and joyful
rest.

[East River End]

my eyes saw for the first time
on the east river drive a body
frozen on the street with newspapers
covered in ice beside it. I shivered
standing in the oddly accusing wind
waiting with the dead for the police.
my eyes saw for the first time pity in
that lonely death, shame for the better
off, and little in the wicked silence
about the meek inheriting the earth.
sleep did not peacefully come that
evening just Lazarus haunting me
with the image of that frozen homeless
man, dead!

[The Wall]

how long ago was it you
wrote on the schoolyard

wall a dream. we have seen
it grow old with the years in

dimming light, talked about it
at seasonal pray altars, and

remembered it in sleep. last
week underneath the weight

of labored days an old man
was on his knees in front of

it raising a bottle of spirits to
you, privately. we saw the

hospital nurse stop for a look
with a small group of dancing

psychiatric patients who weep
more frequently than smile, and

they were motionless in front of
it. all who have a look at your wall

are voiceless here and stand quietly
like students practicing for a school

play. the past is never lost even on
the most clouded day whenever we move

through the streets of the block to stand in front
of your dream scribbled wall. when you come

back to the block someday, we will tell you about
the many ways this wall enchanted us with hope,

laughter, friendship and love.

[Another Country]

they called the neighborhood another
country though the newspapers have
suggested a dozen other things. the
names of those who live there give
them away like their broken English
speech, the jobs held that keep piling
in memory like a closet full of shoes, the
schools teaching English to the kids, and
all the churches speaking in a clearly
foreign tongue. their worn clothes and
buttoned tight shirts have something to
tell even when the rest of the city is not
listening. look. see them. don't be so
blind.

[Brown River]

the brown sluggish river moves
across the earth with the wind riding
on its back around twisting turns to
a lost paradise with wild birds inviting
itinerants in flight. in the low trees
red-billed pigeons astonished by a
border fence, watch us laying in the
grass with fever chills, imagining
the footprints others left in fields,
to help us see the walk not taken by
ugly tyrants with nasty sins. we expect
to see angels skilled in secrets appear
in our sleep to help us race to the far
cities that thicken us with dreams. we
look for a cloud like the one that guided
ancient Israelites across a dessert to life
on another land, believing our shuffling
tongues will find a way to clearly speak
about hands trembling in the dark, the
cemeteries of the slain, and this new
life expanding slow, and certain—come
to the fields to feel the drifting weight of
these things.

[Sugarcane]

in the summer, kids sit around the stoop
chewing on sugarcane, talking of Latino life

in their corner of the city. mothers walk
past smiling telling the sticky lipped friends

the Lord's truth will come about with good
news, soon. the sugarcane kids have sat hungry

at table for days, searched for their names
in strange school halls, castoff gentle faces

of innocence with tears, and seen the bones of sons
and daughters turned to ash. listen: have you looked

at the desolate rooms they live in so far from the sweet
talk of a God who loves? have you heard the hate

thrown their way for being different from people who
contemptuously parade their freedom in white sheets? have

you ever caught the poor boys laugh, their sisters playfully
skip, and their grandmothers say prayer? one day these

kids will demand you explain what you did to strip
your lips of silence, to confess your shame, to speak of

worlds where life and tenderness are beaten thin. stop
thinking about the God imagined at church, sit with

the sugarcane kids and lean in the direction of their
yearning for life.

[Walk Around the Lake]

a little turtle takes sun on the lake
shore for nobody. wordless stones

keep company with her the happy
long day. two girls with mauve ribbons

in black hair walk past giggling about the
little creature living in a box that is a sign like

them of God's doing. I could not help thinking
this agent of the lake who spied my steps

approaching the land's edge knows the
sweet secrets that rise from the depths. how

long can this moment last? When gone will
it be lost forever? a bird wings repeatedly

above the critters dainty head, she keeps the
same calm, enjoying the bliss of time in the

warmth of a daystar—with a low voice I call
out peace surrounds today.

[March with Us]

on the protest march the peaceful witnesses
that walked the half-dark streets began to weep
when shots from a sniper's gun pressed

through space to enter the bodies of blameless
cops. in the tragic light of an evil that
had no use for God, a hell-ringing deliverer

of hate, a psychopathic young man ruled by
the grave, killed. Mother Mary can you see
from your remote home how our eyes today

tear? Do you hear our screams refusing
to become mere dust? Do you truly get our
pleas rising from the hateful fires of this most

tragic and terrifying day? When we drop to
our knees will you attend to the sobbing speech
that bitterly chokes words seeking to tell how

prejudiced hearts swell the world with misery
and death? Will you help us to explain to the
children, friends and family of these men why

they met an untimely end? Lady in heaven
turn to look our way and help us find a
way to create a life together in peace.

[Exit Wound]

I walked up the street to the
gathered crowd hearing words

tossed about that the world will
end one day with fire. they were

grimly spoken without alarm, heavy
to carry in the march, distant from

the sighs and tears that make our
pretty hearts love, adrift from the

real menace to life and everything
we adore—that monstrous thing

named hate. the hour is not too late
I thought to raise a flaming torch instead

to find the ground the angels tread in the
name of everlasting love, to make the

worst in us submit beneath the mild light
of stars to the watchman with the kingdom

beat for such a time as this. I whispered
to the lady beside me talking the story of

her son, after all the words are said this pallid
world will end not by fire, but with the brilliance

of love—she smiled.

[They Tremble to Sleep]

the voice came from the bedroom
door open, calling out in the evening
silence the names of children in another
room, full of life like the trees in the little
park with leaves not yet fallen, inviting
sleepy imaginations to adjust to sounds of
tenderness and love. the boys with arms
intertwining listened to the words drop
in their room yet wondered what would come
next? how could they tell if this was the voice
of a father's love or words again stalking them
in the night before delivering grief? one child
got on his knees looked up toward the ceiling
and whispered Lord burst into my little room
and offer the shadows of this filthy place
the dearest tender life. it got very quiet in the
apartment, no more calling out from the other
bedroom, the next morning the father who
shouted in the dark was gone and life in the
apartment became like a thousand others on the
block.

[Summer Break]

in the spare time of a summer day
I walked to the corner shop that sold

Spanish speaking soul food featuring
parts of pig—*cuchifrito!* the food

place had a flashy sign above its door and
papered specials pasted to the window,

in the colorful slang the kids on the block
learned long before setting foot into public

school 66. in front of the store, *Papo* was
changing the inner tube on his red bike, the

one with a new banana seat and tasseled
butterfly handlebars, taking frequent breaks

to chew on a *pastelillo*—a turnover type thing
only without fruit inside that the English side

of New York has rarely come to the block to
taste. longing to touch the two-wheeled thing

with sunlight bouncing off its rims, I came out
of the shop with coconut juice, handed it to

my highly mobile friend with one hand, and
used the other to pet the gorgeous handlebars like

a magic lamp about to grant a wish. we grew
loud in conversation searching up and down the

street for scenes to make us laugh, checking out
the weekend grown-ups preparing for a night of

sin, feeling the warm wind behind our necks like
a light breath, and pulling summer around our

shoulders like two kids real glad to be on school
break.

[The Fire Escapes]

when I walk the sidewalks of the city,
I see the fire escapes with the faces

of the kids who stared high above the
bustling street, I hear laughter swinging

from the zigzag appendages, and witness
bodies using drop ladders to right themselves

with exercises not for the cautious gym class
of school. these kids who never joined a sports

club, saw the Boy Scouts a hobby for the rich,
could climb to the top floor on metal steps faster

than heaven could fall on the heads of all the shoe
shine boys working the boulevard corners. I prefer

having their happy and stubborn expressions enter
my head on these city walks, to feel their mysterious

truth breaking in, to pause beneath the fire escapes
with a piece of memory hollering the names of all

the games that offered them pleasure, gladness and
peace. I bet the future will be freed by colorful

fire escapes crowded with the glimmering faces of
poor city kids who believe this world with its purest

dreams will keep its mouthful of promises to them.

[The Flower Pot]

I was sitting on the bottom step of the stoop,
the one with names carved on it, looking

up at the moonlight spreading across a dark
sky, thinking about all the things Sonia

yelled out the window, while she arranged
a vase on the sill to rest her dreams despite

the absence in it of flowers. the precious
pot she carefully placed above the messy

street no doubt meant more to her than the
broken light divinity so carefully practiced

sharing on the block. I wondered how many
times Sonia would come back to the window

to cast her fragile regrets to the weary breeze,
to forget about the ladies that close in with

their wretched gossip, to recall days of shared
love, words, and all those things? I wondered

how long before night again would come to her
with caressing hands to make her laugh, dance

and passionately feel joy? I leaned a little
further back on the step declaring the name of

the second floor harlot in my head convinced Sonia
could make a thousand Angels confuse their ways

and an absent minded God offer nothing less than
candid grace—so gossip ladies hush!

[Dead End Street]

do you hear the grown men sobbing
in their elderly mothers' arms filled

with the sorrow that only comes with
the reality of their children flattened

in a world of intolerance and hate? can
you see the Spanish writing in each tear

expressing bitter tales in the land of the
free? did you listen by the grave of the

little boy taken by a stray bullet on the
block, see these tearful men try to bind up

their hearts, and touch their trembling
sad hands? I have listened, touched and

wept with them. when I talk of it the carriers
of the sharp knives of hatred call me sassy, among

other things, and tell me with enjoyment shut up
and let them weep. who will know the desolation

in these grown men's hearts, their lessons of love,
their need for change, their longing for the justice

that is always far? I won't be quiet about these
souls weeping around me and I will curse heaven too

for failing to listen.

[The Factory Floor]

a woman named Ana just started
work at the costume jewelry factory
after spending weeks practicing at

home how to put glue on the tip of
a toothpick to place in tiny settings
where fake diamonds are positioned

to rest. the girl living in apartment
2-B, born just ten blocks from the
tenement, who speaks good English

and only sings in Spanish, a survivor
of the public school that kept all its
students in the dark, invited Sonia to

take the job. they ride the subway to
work each morning talking about the
cries of other woman on the factory floor

for whom bread is dear and bringing up
how many of the ladies bear witness to a
world the foreman warns them never on

the job to speak. we have all been here
before, tossed around the city wasteland,
sitting on the assembly line with life slowly

becoming in the middle of things just dust.
before day turns into a disillusioning sorrow,
Ana with her eyes made from the sweetest

corn, found a way to make joy pour for
private moments of peace, which other
workers learned. Ana simply began her

days with simple prayer produced by the
belief that the tears that Jesus wept for a

city are too dropped for her!

[Works of Love]

it was well into the late afternoon
hour, when the birds began to retreat

to the branches of drooping trees, and
the sky complained of the blazing sun,

that I began wondering about the works
of love. in the alley next to the stoop, I heard

the persecuted voices of dark-skinned men
conversing about the bored Christians in

the church up the street who are never moved
by the way the world keeps driving wood posts

into the ground to put people like them on
the lynching tree. they talked out loud about

never hoping for love, the promises of help
not kept, and the constant weeping from being left

to wrestle with abandonment dressed with the
thinnest armor of God. my hobbling heart listened

to their words describe the highest work of love was
God in the alley alongside of them, the maker nailed

to death on wood, the Lord who dwells in tenements,
keeps watch over lofty piety, and with a gentle voice

says follow me. I sat on the stoop all day thinking of
the works of love, the consequence of adoring faith,

the daily blows against God, and finally realized the
ancient shepherd in the alley waits for me.

[Street Light]

gaily the streetlights shine this
evening with the gentle falling

snow, while in the distance is
heard the alluring songs of the

little storefront church packed
with bodies of the least upon

the earth. sounds rest in
my ears leading me past all the

daily judgement halls to quietly
rest with those who see Angels

in clouds, light in darkness
coming, and the Lord of Good in

everything. on this wintry night,
providence comes to me in the

silent spaces between sounds, in
the hunch of heaven within, and

the lined faces of children who
leave their footprints in the white

powdered sidewalk laughing in their
remarkable worlds. I lean closer into

the images of night, light casing
this block, and accept the resonant

being that makes shadows fall.

[Fourth of July]

I could hear the explosions from
the rooftop and see the night sky

bursting colors to celebrate the
weight of the freedom we breathe.

we watched the blazing sky offering
beauty to our eyes, securely writing

our chocolate names, the questions
we dare speak, and the history we too

have from the beginning bleed. I heard
the seasons shouting on independence

night on Saint Mark's Place, saw them
holding the bitter politicians by the hair,

making them empty their pockets of hate,
and placing them in front of all the broken

voices that have made our nation great. in
the smoky peace, I thought of all the times

the wind was shattered by the young bodies
from the block who lost their lives in foreign

wars, how folks like Trump mispronounce
their names, and discount their sacrifice. I

fell to my knees weeping like a cloud full
of rain and pleaded for God to grant in life

above the grave, love in the harshest days,
fading scorn in every State, and the sweet

warming flames of America for us. I prayed
for loveliness to ignite in the angriest hearts to

make them shout with us loud enough to split
the dark that America is our sweet home 'til

final dust!

[Stand]

I have walked many streets in
cities, villages and towns, slept

the hard benches of gloomy parks,
eaten scraps with wretched Spanish

speaking drunks, tasted cheap wine
on corners the good folk with dreams

always missed, inhaled the stench of
dope shooting galleries set up in gutted

buildings that no longer hear the loud
voices of children thundering with play.

in my arms, I have held the bodies of
friends who gasped a last breath, gave a

brother one horrible day to the earth, seen
coffins hit the ground with too many children

in last sleep. I have listened to the wailing
coming from windows where grandmothers

sit, seen their shivering rosaries dangle from
the ledges, and the dark never lift. I have

spent many days in places of violence and
hate shouting for peace, demanded milk

and honey to drip, caught tiny glimmers of
light between the days, and wrestled with

yesterday and what will come to roam around
in me—so here I stand!

[The Morning News]

the smell of bus exhaust made its
way into the restaurant, and the morning
paper with sanitized stories of drone

strikes in Pakistan, gang wars up the
block, and the bakery closing after
fifty years, waited at the tables for hungry

guests. the big picture that was already in
possession of our names was hiding beneath
in the lines between the text, waiting

to be split open like a knife wound hand in a
kitchen begging to be cured. I could see the
patrons of the place focused on the sports pages

reporting millionaires at play, enjoying the gossip in
stories they half-believed, and barely feeling a thing.
with eyes a little wider, I thought they would not miss

the news reported on page twelve of the kid who
walks the streets with his arms around himself disguised
he says like love, or the story on page twenty-three

of the mother who cries for her dead child everyday
standing on the corner of Fox Street. the other breaking
news is something to learn, the students at P.S. 66 have

names, they want playgrounds with working swings,
teachers who clear the dust from books, and brave their eager
faces with education without end. before the breakfast

hour ended, I wondered whether or not the morning news
readers would find the last page of the paper that reports the
future will not wait for them to finally get around to see the

things that need change.

[Politics]

politics that talks a thousand
lies and makes us bleed will

never fix the hungry streets,
the family without a home, the

overseas wars, the debt economy,
the jobless who no longer speak,

addicts on the corners, the rancorous
men who want more heads, the sky

that weeps for the tortured, maimed,
exploited and loathed. the politicians

who cannot hear many voices sing O say
can you see, by the dawn's early light,

who feel their stomachs turn when border
children draw near, and fear the ringing in

their ears of Black chants for lives that matter
will never make a nation great. politics to make

us great will fall in love with every name, walk
with light in hand, find beauty in a colored land,

and deliver equality, freedom and justice to every
one who lives.

[The Bus]

in the cold rain the people on
the block are rushing to the bus

stops wearing hefty bags for
coats. you can feel the chill on

their tired faces, the confusion
in their eyes about the group of

boys arrested for sitting on church
steps, the ways they question how

democracy can never be a product
of fear. it's a shame that the rest of

the country does not know the hard
working poor carry more weight

than Atlas did night stars. the
girl no longer young wonders out

loud with a friend about God dropping
in on the bus stop after listening to

prayers downtown in the fancy churches
offering carefully wrapped friendliness

to people of means. more dark faces keep
inching in to the stop, the chatting grows

a little louder to warm the coldness on
their cheeks, then someone yells the bus.

[A Short Walk]

walk with me on this moonlit path
beyond the houses with bruised hearts,
broken windows, restless dreams and
muttering tongues. stand with me on
the corner until the silver fog shakes
open the eyes of junkies nodding out
in the hidden corners of night. drop your
questions on the rooftops we will visit
to find street kids who measure life in
spoons and spend days listening to the
voices of friends who dance with death.
pause with me under the lighting street lamp
where grandmothers gather and share with
them your thoughts about how to begin change.
weep with me standing on the yellowing newspapers
scattered in the vacant lots that never say an honest
word of this forsaken place you've seen. at the end
of the walk, rest with me for a little while by the fountain
in the park on the other side of the avenue to sing Lord
move us nearer to truth.

[The Orange]

the Nuyorican boy was munching
an orange on the street just pulled

from a number 2 brown bag, which
his cousin always liked to use to sniff

glue. you could see the fruit in his hand
was filling him with more comfort than

inhaled paste or the words spoken by the
priest with a crooked tongue who walked

past smiling. sometimes he wakes at three
in the morning to the sound of sirens and the

loud snore of fire trucks passing beneath his
window that makes him think of jumping out

of bed to slay dragons. when he can't fall back
to sleep, he imagines putting his feet down on

the perilous paths down by the East River swollen
with shrubs, roamed by tiny creatures who never

see the block, to the train bridge to sit with
collected neighborhood dreams. I stopped to

look at him the last time he ate oranges on the
corner, pretending in my head this place was the

Garden of Eden that the two of us would trade
without a single question for a taste of heaven far

off.

[Sunday]

Sunday morning with a little dream
awake in a chair with the sun rising
without a sound and the holy mystery
come for a visit from Palestine with the
wind to suckle our needy souls. paradise
what can it be? Enduring love? the painful
sacrifice of blood? to live without mistakes?
the best of earth known to us? the lips joined
in love? the sleepless hope of every heart that
asks from whence it came and whither shall it go?
the rose blooming in the dark? the unspoken part
of day? Paradise I wonder?

[The Subway Station]

the next time the landlord cuts
heat in your building, come with

me to the Simpson Street subway
station, where there is a room with

a heater that one morning ate my
fake leather jacket. we can stay

warm in there for hours, count the
coming trains, talk with strangers

in Spanish all day, and peer through
a cracked door window at the old men

who have taken the train for years to
work downtown. we can rap about

the latest songs played at the parties on
the block not meant to educate or save,

the night Willy drank the cheapest wine
two dollars could buy from the corner liquor

store to throw it up at Margaritas' party like a
teen who discovered bars in jail for the first

time. we can spend a few hours gossiping
about the day Joseph argued with the block

priest insisting he never read a thing in the bible
saying Jesus was thinking about dying for him, the

Sunday mass never made his skin tingle, and the
last fire of Pentecost that visited the block began

in a storefront church that took a whole building to the
ground—God no longer for sale. the point is come

with me to the subway station to stay warm for free,
talk about what you have seen, share your ideas like

a flower does its colors, then go back home tonight with
warmth for the freezing family flat.

[War]

before the candles in the hallway
blew out, when the doors in the

building began to open for another
day of work, the girlfriend came to

pray for Manny who didn't like the
orders to ship to Viet Nam, hid behind

the steps from the Military police that
came looking for him on the block, and

dropped dead on a dope overdose. he
never liked the flags that dripped with

blood hanging on the fire escapes of
the apartments where mothers pulled

curtains to cry, alone. he hated how the
Pentecostals spent so much time with their

bibles in prayer, while all the poor kids on
the block joined the Marines to get a step up,

and were quickly pounded into war graves.
he told a bunch of us how he detested the

world the sorry politicians ambitious for empire
construed with war, hunger, poverty and hate. now

we light candles on the very spot Manny passed
away cursing the day he left this place and damning

those who send our children into combat far away
to make themselves quite rich.

[Darling]

see me on the corner empty of
trees where I will wait with a well
practiced hello sitting on my lips.

find me standing next to the old domino
players who have outlived the small string
of years they were granted at birth. I will

be watching the wind roll scraps of newspaper
along the sidewalk thinking about the Spanglish
histories they ignored, with a very foolish smile

on my face inspired by the thought you will
arrive with a part of me already in you. I will
whisper a prayer when your figure is drawing

near from the distance, take your hand for a
stroll along Southern Boulevard to the only
florist on the block, and together we will pick

little roses with naked hearts, lift them up to the
stars, and in a gentle embrace capable of melting
the sky allow our lips to meet. no one knows you

on the block like me, the look in your mild eyes,
the tenderness you leave behind simply walking
along the street, your whispered songs floating in

the spaces of my soul, the bells your laughter rings
that call on divinity to dare a peek, and the boundless
love you share with those abandoned by care. hurry

to the corner so I can tell you nothing in the world
turns to dust, sadness stumbles to the earth, and
the future calls out to us.

[Caged Bird]

I tried to put my mother's little bird
in the cage the night it flew out to

visit all three rooms of the apartment.
I chased it about saying its name and

a whole bunch of prayers in the sudden
dark, *Pancho, ven*—the bird could not

speak a word of English. with the windows
tightly shut, I put seed in my hand to lure

the winged house mate closer, and by love's
grace get him back in his truest home. I

sat down in the living room on the plastic
slip covered sofa that on Summer nights

would get up with you to play, thinking
how foolish to keep this little air creature

in a cage when it really wants to fly around
free. with the bird still soaring around the rooms,

and my world still in panic, it became clear that
freedom in a cage only opens doors of nonsense.

the bird did not take the seed from me, then the
idea occurred to wait for mother to make it home

from factory work, to propose she consider what in
a thousand years would never enter her head—lets open

the windows for this *pajarito* to fly away into a bigger
freer world. I waited in the dark hoping mother would

agree with me and see for herself Gabriel lunging
from the dark to blow his final trumpet for us.

[Lost]

he stands on the corner loved
by the wind that sometimes makes
him shiver. in a pocket of his torn

pants, he keeps a charm given to him
by a *Santería* priest at the Botanica on
Prospect Avenue run like a spiritual home

depot with shelves stacked with oils, herbs,
amulets, cleaning fluids, varieties of candles
and believe it or not dragons blood. the day

he received it a lady was visiting the priest
complaining that her son who believed himself a
snake, would eat his rice and beans slithering

on the kitchen floor, while sticking his tongue
in and out—the priest gave her something to
put in the boys shoes. like some old man

alone in tears, his young regretful eyes survey
the sidewalk that swallows the dust kicked up
by those who walk by yet never see him. after

the sun withdraws to other worlds, old family
pain climbs slowly into his head making him
wonder when the hours in this spell become

life will raise the ancient cup. in another pocket,
he keeps a picture of his mother with the names of
two siblings written on it to remember there is a door

at the end of loss. last week, he was still standing
on that corner asking why the Great potter left him
for spilled clay and demanding to know when the

millions of tears he has shed will turn into the kind
hour of release.

[The Fire]

the building was on fire,
the old women standing

on the sidewalk whispered
shameless words they never

admitted knowing. Shorty's
father came running into the

street wearing boxers, and still
firmly holding a can of Schaeffer

beer. the pigeons scattered from
the rooftop to other roosts where

fire could not scorch them and
smoke smelled far. the people

talked about how relocation in this
ruin would add other scars, and wished

that night was nothing more than fiction.
they saw few possessions and things cherished

turn to ash. the holy sentences Father Rossi
spoke out on the sidewalk could not keep them

from swallowing bitter tears. the children who
shouted the end of the world, while crying for

toys forever lost, smiled when Victor's grandfather
showed up holding a Polaroid camera to take pictures

in the thickening air. the old man posed families
for shots with the building behind him in flames

and he passed around a little bottle of holy water
rescued from a night table by his bed telling everyone

to place a pious drop on their heads to give thanks
for being held in saving arms of *papa Dios*.

[Recalling]

there he sits on the corner shining
shoes brightly on the spot where
questions never find a pure reply
and his name is carefully etched
on the sidewalk. just yesterday
he thought of home thousands of
miles away where the soldiers herded
people with dogs, the dead cooled in
the hot sun, the politicians crept away
from cries, and the common people
fled. words do not come easy from
that inward place bullying him now
with madness.

[The Talk]

on this bend of the street sly old
women chew bread and when the

pious look away sip it down with
a little rum. when they hear the

church bells ring inviting the filthy
and the fair, the dogs barking in

the shade, and the neighbors tongues
begin to sing, they love after another

tiny sip to shout from apartment windows
a dark cloud will settle on hatred's

head. I visited Angel's grandmother one
night begging her to tell me stories, the delicate

fables in Spanish describing her days wandering
the streets, the journey that brought her to these

shores, and why she settled on this block
decorated with a broken English clock. she

dropped a gentle laugh in the dim living room,
and I let woe scatter on the linoleum floor beneath

her feet. she sat beside me with a photo album,
her eyes searching for truth, the men and women

she loved on its pages, their secrets guarded in her
heart, and intricate memories near—the night could

not have been more beautiful for talk.

[The Bronx]

listening to the symphony Sid show was
reason enough to live in the Bronx, the sounds

of the latest salsa playing on the street to make
the air stop for a dance on the stoop, a fit place

for children, animals, former prisoners of war,
and grown-ups paying for their sins. we never

believed it a dangerous place to live, no hazard
signs ever appeared in the stores, the tenements,

the schools, police cars, trains, buses, churches
or parks, just simple people suffering their days

without ever saying a thing. each year people left
behind joys, sorrows, stories full of gestures turned

now to dust. you never heard complaining of life
scorched beyond recognition, working mothers

too bent for kids, nor people who never bothered
to sing. the tired hands were reason enough never

to say goodbye to these streets, the moments we
laughed at death with its black cape, when paintings

of everyday life settled in memory to fill hearts.
this place is reason enough to keep searching with

light from broken stars and Angels posing dead
for the truth that gave us a first delicious breath.

[The Book]

in the old pages of a favorite book
with eyes made of the finest corn

words once read on the windy shores
of the sea made her weep. she greeted

the early Spring with its tales, listened
to the whistling breeze flipping over its

pages, thought of drunkards walking
on the beach, while wondering about the

questions in the text that measured life
for her. she slept peacefully at night

with the old book at her side with its
dog ear marks gently smoothed to near

perfection before dropping into the world
of dreams. she grew old with that scroll

that lacked a single high sentence yet said
more than a thing or two about truth. she

kept the book on an altar in her bedroom,
lighted a candle behind it every night, and

remembered to give thanks for aging with it.
her corn made eyes always cried from reading

but not a single tear came with sadness nor fear
for her clay life declining with time. I now have

it, and when I lie alone, reach for it.

[The Game]

I still remember our first game of stick
ball with a pink Spaulding and an old mop

stick on Fox Street, the chatty-Kathy doll your
little sister sat with on the stoop talking up

a world of English the kids just in from the
island could not understand, the look in your

eyes of truth tainted by the realization that in
this new South Bronx world nothing for you

would be the same. I will never forget the day
you walked into the bodega to buy a can of spray

paint you said to gracefully write lines on school
yard walls, the number two train and in front of

the Fort Apache police station explaining with the
drops of tint you are here. you loved to hear the

knocking of the church bells that made people in
the neighborhood rise up for time, for some reason

you always bowed your head to invite a blessing on
the day, and those of us around you swore the look

in your eyes was papered with the sweetest Orchids
the forests back home grew. unbearably long ago,

I wonder what has become of you, did you sew by
hand another life, did the years escort you to the

brightest shapes of love, will you ever come back
to the block to tell us about the many ways and places

you cried to be fulfilled—I hope soon.

[Walking Home]

sometimes walking home from
the block late at night I stop by the

Jewish bakery to look at the sweets
left in the window display. there is

always a light on in the closed shop
that shines all night much like the

candles that burn constantly at the
church. I often thought the sick

who are taken to the altar for blessing
and prayer in dark churches would heal

faster showing up while it's still dark in
front of Moshe's to bite into one of his

colorful treats. they would see children
skipping off to school, old women sweeping

the street, old men remembering scars
formed, a few stray dogs crossing the

yellow cab road, and lean into the huge
hum of a new day pleased to listen to its

noise. they'd smell the odors of the
sweetest kitchen filling the worn places

they strain to understand—Moshe's bakery
open or closed will always be an exquisite

place to be.

[Talk]

we moved to the city with a new tongue, each word laced with the mysteries stitched on the hill tops where language was invented, our sounds casting clouds of confusion for the English only residents on the block, the word *silencio* providing each of us a space to hide from the babblers of hate. we moved to the block to see an end to village sighs, whistling serpents thrilling us with final sleep, to find a place where the sign of the cross would once again dismiss time that never permits the dawn. we moved to a building with enormous rooms that uttered the fine stories of the world's simple clay that amazed residents with light to have their dreams out. after these many years, our English speaking kids walk with everlasting frowns affected by those who toss in front of them the phrase *go home strangers this land will never be a place for your brown face, shelter you with freedom or let spics like you live in peace*—wrong!

[The Pigeon-Man]

I sat on the rooftop where the
pigeon-man was flying his birds

with a flag on a long bamboo pole
over the streets. the tenderness of

humanity was always visible in his
eyes and though I never heard a bird

say God it was clear to my childish
ways the gentleness of the ancient

word was there. the pigeon-man loved
to sit with his birds in the coop, feed

them with his hands, and wear huge
smiles watching the majestic flight

of feathers above the tattered Bronx
tenements. he was most certainly

a rare breed on the block who could
talk for hours about the swoop and

glide of his pigeons, and I never did
mind getting lost on the rooftop with

him. heaven could not topple to
our corner of the earth a clearer

image of love than that delivered
by the pigeon-man's birds with their

blessed airy gift of light.

[The Choir]

sometimes the choir sings loud
enough for pedestrians to hear

walking down Hoe Avenue holding
hands, while careening cop cars

pass, and children in the apartments
are ransacking refrigerators for

anything to eat. they walk busy
with their own troubles not seeing

Sonia on the church steps already
offering a glimpse of the God that

dwells with us disguised like a street
walker, a store clerk, a beautician,

park drunks, homeless mothers, angry
old men, high school drop outs, strung

out teens, incarcerated youth, soldiers
deceased, and grandmothers sitting on

the stoops. the pedestrians who carry
the church choir's harmonies to the subway

station hardly ever peek into the doorways
favored by the penniless who would no doubt

help them to see the warning signs inside their
half-finished dreams. sometimes the choir sings

loud enough to let a little bit of heaven slip in
to the places needing to be seriously touched

up.

www.ingramcontent.com/pod-product-compliance
Lightning Source LLC
Chambersburg PA
CBHW070456090426
42735CB00012B/2573